ROMANCE MONOGRAPHS, INC.
Number 8

ENCINA AND VIRGIL

ROMANCE MONOGRAPHS, INC.

Number 8

ENCINA AND VIRGIL

BY

JAMES A. ANDERSON

UNIVERSITY, MISSISSIPPI

ROMANCE MONOGRAPHS, INC.

1 9 7 4

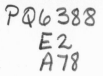
COPYRIGHT © 1974

BY

ROMANCE MONOGRAPHS, INC.

P. O. Box 7553

UNIVERSITY, MISSISSIPPI 38677

PRINTED IN SPAIN

I.S.B.N. 84-399-2158-6

DEPÓSITO LEGAL: V. 1.829 - 1974

ARTES GRÁFICAS SOLER, S. A. - JÁVEA, 28 - VALENCIA (8) - 1974

Library of Congress Cataloging in Publication Data

Anderson, James A.   1934-
    Encina and Virgil.

    (Romance monographs, no. 8)
    Includes bibliographical references.

    1. Encina, Juan del, 1468-1529?-Aesthetics. 2. Encina, Juan del, 1468-1529?
—Style. 3. Vergilius Maro, Publius—Translations, Spanish. I. Title.

PQ6388.E2A78   871'.01   74-75722

ACKNOWLEDGMENT

Many people have helped me in my work on Encina. It is impossible to thank them adequately. For their enthusiasm and curiosity in my work, rather than for their abundant kindness and erudition (which is known everywhere), I should like especially to thank Professor Raymond S. Willis of Princeton and Professor Emeritus Ramón Martínez-López of Texas. In particular I want to express my gratitude to Professor Luis Monguió of Berkeley. Publication of this monograph was made possible by a NDEA Title IV Fellowship through The University of Texas. Part of the time allowed me by a University Research Institute Award was devoted to several sections of the present study. To the members of my Department and the administration of The University of Texas who aided me in both the awards and the monograph, I am deeply grateful.

TABLE OF CONTENTS

INTRODUCTION

IN THE FOLLOWING PAGES I WILL STUDY ASPECTS OF JUAN DEL ENCINA's poetic aesthetics as they are seen in his translations of Virgil's eclogues (called the *Bucólicas* by Encina). It is not meant, at this time, to be a study of Encina's translations *per se*, but rather further observation of his artistic procedure. This can be seen clearly, I feel, as we watch Encina, line by line so to speak, follow Virgil closely or drift away from him. When he is obviously drifting—and deliberately—we may perceive more clearly his idea of the beautiful (although sometimes we will be unable to explain it); when he is staying close to the letter and the tone of Virgil we may perceive the extent of his technical accomplishments.

I do not wish, either, to enter into a general discussion of Encina's Virgilian eclogues, except as this will appear on occasion in the three comparisons. These translations have, for many reasons, often been discussed; but they have not ever been studied in much detail. The generally accepted idea is that they are loose imitations, but it will be seen that this is not so by any means.

Most definitely I do not wish—rather, cannot—enter the field of Virgil's poetry. I am trying to look at Virgil through Encina's eyes, and those statements I do make about Virgil will be obvious and general, and I will have been guided to make them by having reacted first to Encina's version of Virgil's poetry.

In the matter of selection of Virgil's texts I am not being critical, but am accepting the word of people who should know, and have used the original Latin text supplied by E. V. Rieu in his translation of the eclogues. I have also used the Loeb edition, and an eighteenth-century edition, with many notes, which came my way by chance and which has proved to be very useful. The text of Encina's translations is that of the *Cancionero* of 1496 (facs. ed.)[1]. As for the Virgil that Encina used, I have been assured that of all the classic authors Virgil is the one whose texts have always been most "clean" and "complete," and the chances are very great that Encina's Virgil would correspond almost exactly to any modern one that was prepared with reasonable care, and this seems to be the case.

Encina states in his dedication to the Catholic Kings: "¡O, quántas vezes me paro a pensar, desconfiando de mi ingenio, quién me puso en este trabajo, aviendo otros muchos que muy mejor que yo lo pudieran tomar!" (fo. [31]ᵛ). I suspect that Nebrija might well have supplied Encina with an excellent copy of the text (Nebrija provided his own edition of Virgil some years later, and it seems he had prepared an earlier edition, now lost, for students at Salamanca).

The two dedications (one to the Catholic Kings, one to the Prince) are very interesting explanations of Encina's motivations (and qualifications) for making this translation, and should be read. (See Appendix and Note 12.)

I will study Encina's version in this comparative way with some leisure, but it goes without saying that I have not exhausted every possibility in this analysis. My choice of eclogues here is not in itself significant, except for the fourth, which was chosen because it is in *arte mayor* (which is an indication that Encina himself singled it out).[2] At first it was my intention to consider all ten of the eclogues in this manner, and that may still be done, but in a more limited scope, as part of a careful edition of the eclogues. For the present, a study of three eclogues handles

---

[1] Juan del Encina, *Cancionero*, facs. ed. [Salamanca, 1496], intro. Emilio Cotarelo y Mori (Madrid, 1928); I have resolved the abbreviations, supplied accents, and added some modern punctuation. Encina's own punctuation remains, as will be noted. Other references to Encina's texts are to this ed. Virgil, *The Pastoral Poems*, tr. E. V. Rieu (Harmondsworth, Middlesex, 1954). Also for Virgil, *Eclogues, Georgics, Aeneid* ed. and tr. H. Rushton Fairclough (London, 1965); *Works*, I (London, 1763), no ed. or translator given. Other translations of the Eclogues are those of Bernardo Pulci (Florence, 1481) and Guillaume Michel de Tours (Paris?, 1516). Both are literal translations; the French is in the manner of the *grands rhétoriquers*.

[2] It is, of course, significant that the fourth eclogue had been considered part of the Christian tradition. See note 9.

sufficiently the question of Encina's aesthetics with which I am concerned.

In a general way, I would like to mention three impressions I have about Encina's translations: *1)* they are intended as translations for people who could not read Virgil—it being Encina's belief that he was, in fact, writing as Virgil would have done in Spain at that time ; *2)* they exist as a series of ten poems in praise of the monarchy, and are readable for that reason alone ; *3)* they are serious translations made for the special delectation of those whose knowledge of Virgil's eclogues was intimate and whose love of Spanish poetry was great. This last consideration is one that will only be touched on here, but which offers promise of much fruitful investigation.

FIRST ECLOGUE

VIRGIL'S FIRST ECLOGUE IS A STUDY IN CONTRASTS, and—its other virtues aside—is appealing and intriguing owing to its somewhat mysterious innuendoes and its vagueness as the two shepherds intertwine their speeches. Meliboeus speaks of a "man like a god" who brought him happiness and liberty; Tityrus must go into exile because of "the trouble all about him." While we may make applications of all this to specific historical facts, Virgil (apparently) does not; Encina, following in the body of his poem the vagueness of Tityrus, explains in his *Argumento* the specific causes for his misery, while making explicit in the poem the identity of Virgil's uncertain liberator. It is, of course, the King—to be more precise, the Catholic Kings, Ferdinand and Isabella.

...en esta primera égloga se introduzen dos pastores razonándose el uno con el otro como que a caso se encontraron, uno llamado Melibeo que habla en persona de los cavalleros que fueron despojados de sus haziendas por ser rebeldes conjurando con el rey de Portugal que de Castilla fue alançado; y con él anduvieron amontados y corridos, perseverando en su contumacia; y el otro pastor, que Titiro [sic] fue llamado habla en nombre de los que en arrepentimiento vinieron y fueron restituydos en su primero estado; y va tocando el tiempo que reynó el señor rey don Enrique Quarto, començando su reynar con tanto rigor de justicia que no menos de temido que de poderoso pudiera ser alabado. Mas en el fin atibiando su poder y afloxando su justicia, dio lugar a que en los coraçones de sus súditos, a vanderas desplegadas vicios y robos se apoderassen, para cuyo remedio tan católicos y tan ecelentes Príncipes Dios por su misericordia nos quiso dar. Y agora Titiro [sic] por más lastimar a Melibeo, que era del vando contrario, muestra quanta mejoría y ecelencia lleva la realeza y corte deste nuestro muy vitorioso rey a la de todos los otros, doliéndose por que tan tarde vino en el verdadero conocimiento, y maravillándose en persona del poeta como tuvo atrevimiento para escrevir hazañas de tan alto príncipe, y dando gracias por las mercedes recebidas.

One will note that Encina omits practically entirely the references to Amaryllis, which in Virgil afford a small but important love motive which makes it more difficult to understand the underlying theme or philosophy of the Latin poem (except insomuch as it may be considered a *sine qua non* of pastoral poetry in Virgil's time). It will be noted, also, that Encina will at one time condense Virgil, at another time expand him in a purely formal way (i.e., not textually); perhaps there is some pattern to be observed in Encina's manipulations of the Latin text. In the first exchanges, Meliboeus and Tityrus each speak five lines in Virgil, but in Encina the former speaks three strophes and the latter only two:

MELIBOEUS

Tityre, tu patulae recubans sub tegmine fagi
silvestrem tenui musam meditaris avena:
nos patriae fines et dulcia linquimus arva;
nos patriam fugimus: tu, Tityre, lentus in umbra
formosam resonare doces Amaryllida silvas.

¡Tytiro, quán sin cuydado
que te estás so aquesta haya
bien tendido y rellanado!
Yo triste, descarriado,
ya no sé por do me vaya,
¡ay, Carillo
tañes tú tu caramillo!
No ay quien cordojo te traya.

Yo lazerado, aborrido,
he dexado ya mi tierra;
ando acossado y huydo,
y tú estáste aquí tendido

a sabor por esta sierra
canticando,
por las silvas retumbando;
no tienes quien te dé guerra.

Cantas dos mil cantilenas
de Amarilis tu adamada;
deslindándole tus penas,
tus presiones y cadenas,
tiénesla bien canticada;
con reposo
a la sombra gasajoso
no te das nada por nada.

There is here no basic departure from Virgil's text; as in other instances Encina pays close attention to it, developing the literal meaning as well as the implied or poetical meaning. Thus, departing from Virgil's "recubans" Encina says: "quán sin cuydado / que te estás so aquesta haya / bien tendido y rellanado" in the first strophe, and in the second adds "Tú estáste aquí tendido / a sabor por esta sierra." Similarly, Virgil's implied contrast is made very clear in Encina: "We [I] leave our fatherland and *sweet* fields" (made intense in Virgil through repetition, "linquimus fines patriae" and "fugimus patriam") becomes "yo, triste, descarriado / ya no sé por dó me vaya," "Yo lazerado, aborrido," "Ando acossado y huydo." These feelings are explicit in Virgil only to the extent that the fields Meliboeus is abandoning are *dulcia*. Encina further emphasizes the concept of "recubans" and the later "lentus" in the three final lines of each strophe, lines which are parallel in construction (and which are, it is obvious, "vernacular," i.e., "rustic").

Here, in the translation of a classic writer, Encina avoids all mention of anything that might be considered pagan mythology, something that is a noticeable departure from his other works. (This does not apply to all the Virgilian translations.) Other instances of this avoidance will be indicated. Thus, "meditaris silvestrem *musam*" becomes simply "Tañes tú tu caramillo" and the idea of "*teaching* the woods" (*doces* silvas resonare) becomes simply "por las silvas retumbando." Virgil's sonorous, onomatopoetic construction "lentus in umbra / formosam resonare" is not lost in Encina's version, however, with his lighter, but not less effective

> canticando,
> por las silvas retumbando.

As if to compensate for having removed "pagan" concepts, and lest one be misled by Encina's declaration of writing in "estilo pastoril," it must be noted that he adds, most gratuitously, the nature of the shepherd's love for "formosam Amaryllida," which is the nature of love so often described in courtly poetry during the fifteenth century:

> deslindándole tus *penas*,
> tus *presiones y cadenas*.

TITYRUS

O Meliboee, deus nobis haec otia fecit.
namque erit ille mihi semper deus, illius aram
saepe tener nostris ab ovilibus imbuet agnus.
ille meas errare boves, ut cernis, et ipsum
ludere quae vellem calamo permisit agresti.

> O buen zagal Melibeo,
> quánto bien nos hizo Dios;
> diónos rey de tal asseo
> que todo nuestro desseo
> se nos cumple, juro a ños;
> y le amamos
> tanto que por él rezamos
> primero que no por nos.
>
> El nos dexa andar paciendo
> el ganado por do quiere,
> bien assí como estás viendo
> y estar nos tanto tañendo
> quanto nuestra gana fuere,
> y cantar
> cada qual de buen vagar
> qual cantar por bien tuviere.

Encina remains faithful only to Virgil's last two lines, which are handled in the second strophe. Lines two and three, wherein is found the distinct image of sacrificial offering of a lamb on an altar, are disregarded completely—perhaps less for their pagan overtones than for their too obviously Christian ones. This is done in much the same way Encina changes the emphasis of Virgil's first line, which is the word "deus": [a] God gave us this leisure [and I shall honor him as a God]. This concept of a man-god becomes, very properly, "Quánto bien nos hizo Dios." The rest of the strophe is only faintly reminiscent of the corresponding section of Virgil's poem. (Note Encina's use of "ños" in the set phrase "juro a ños," which rhymes with "nos." This is deliberate, and not merely a typographical error.)

MELIBOEUS

Non equidem invideo; miror magis: undique totis
usque adeo turbatur agris. en, ipse capellas
protinus aeger ago; hanc etiam vix, Tityre, duco.
hic inter densas corylos modo namque gemellos,
spem gregis, ah, silice in nuda conixa reliquit.
saepe malum hoc nobis, si mens non laeva fuisset,
de caelo tactas memini praedicere quercus.
sed tamen, iste deus qui sit, da, Tityre, nobis.

> Embidia no te la tengo,
> mas antes me maravillo
> que por todo allá do vengo
> tienen un temblor muy luengo
> y es muy fuerte el omezillo;
> ¡ay, cuytado!
> con este poco ganado
> ando triste y amarillo.
>
> Apenas puedo aballar
> por los cerros ni los llanos;
> desta cabra he gran pesar,
> que comiença de anaziar;
> no me doy con ella a manos,
> que parió
> y dos mielgos me dexó
> entre aquellos avellanos.
>
> Y pariólos hembra y macho
> que era verlos maravilla,

> do pudiera aver buen cacho
> para en campo sin empacho
> o para vender en villa;
> ¡ay, quán cruda,
> en una peña desnuda
> los parió, que era manzilla!
>
> Muchas vezes he membrança
> del cielo venir señales
> que nos davan figurança
> de la mal aventurança
> de nuestras cuytas y males;
> digo ¡hey!
> ¿quién es ora aquesse rey
> de tan buenos temporales?

This is a balanced translation, two lines of Virgil corresponding approximately to one strophe of Encina. However, several differences will be noted: the contrast between Meliboeus and Tityrus is made in a different way. In Virgil Meliboeus is sick "aeger," while in Encina he is "triste y amarillo," and also in Encina it seems that the emphasis is on the details of a profitable rustic life that Melibeo will have to abandon and the surprise of Meliboeus upon seeing his friend in such serenity in spite of the "turbatur undique" (que por todo allá do vengo / tienen un temblor muy luengo). Another difference is seen in Encina's avoiding pagan superstition, changing the signs from heaven in the form of a struck oak (in some versions that of the unlucky crow) into the general "señales del cielo" (Encina's fourth strophe; Virgil's seventh line). Further difference may be seen in Encina's treatment of Meliboeus' sadness on the loss of the twin lambs. Virgil's "hanc etiam vix duco" becomes much more detailed, much more imagistic if you will, in Encina:

> Apenas puedo aballar
> por los cerros ni los llanos;
> desta cabra he gran pesar,
> que comiença de anaziar,
> no me doy con ella a manos...

Into this development of Virgil's passing reference, Encina also
builds up the concept of "aeger" which was dismissed in his pre-
vious strophe. Instead of Virgil's simple "gemellos, spem gregis"
we have Encina's very elaborated

> Y pariólos hembra y macho,
> que era verlos maravilla
> do pudiera aver buen cacho
> > [i.e., *spem gregis*]
> para en campo sin empacho
> o para vender en villa...

Very surprising is Encina's omission of Meliboeus' statement: "si
mens non laeva fuisset." It seems that Encina's purpose here was
to avoid as many philosophical digressions as possible from what
he considered to be the unifying element of the poem—i.e., the
praise of the King. Thus it was proper for him to develop in
detail the potential attributes of the lost lambs, and to emphasize
through elaboration Meliboeus' weakness; but just as he will not
enter in his version into the love theme, neither will he consider
the spiritual weakness (mens laeva), which might well be consi-
dered an excuse for his behavior.

─ *TITYRUS*

Urbem, quam dicunt Romam, Meliboee, putavi
stultus ego huic nostrae similem, quo saepe solemus
pastores ovium teneros depellere fetus.
sic canibus catulos similes, sic matribus haedos
noram, sic parvis componere magna solebam.
verum haec tantum alias inter caput extulit urbes,
quantum lenta solent inter viburna cupressi.

> O Melibeo, solía
> yo de muy bovo pensar
> la que corte se dezía
> deste rey, que parecía
> aqueste nuestro lugar;
> y en su corte
> que no avía más deporte
> del que acá suelen tomar.

Por estos valles y cerros
do guardamos los pastores
vemos perritos a perros
y a las madres los bezerros
semejar, aunque menores;
bien assí
al lugar en que nací
comparava los mayores.

Tan gran diferencia va
de otras villas y lugares
al lugar do el rey está,
todo te parecerá
qual el plazer con pesares,
bien como es
con el viburno el ciprés,
que acá todos son casares.

The textual variation of Encina's first strophe is understandable. He follows the syntactic pattern set by Virgil more closely than he does on other occasions; thus:

Urbem-Meliboee-putavi-stultus ego-nostrae similem:

Melibeo-bovo-pensar-la corte-parecía nuestro [lugar].

The syntactic similarity, which is quite surprising, is not nearly as strong, however, as the lexical density, especially in view of the fact that Encina handled his lines very delicately, indulging in hyperbaton twice—a technique that is not very frequent in his work. It is true that the hyperbaton is not very startling here (solía yo de muy bovo pensar; la que corte se dezía deste rey) (it is also true that Virgil's syntax is more "Spanish" than is usual). This aspect of Encina's aesthetics may, perhaps, be clarified somewhat by looking more closely at his use of hyperbaton here. The use of it in Latin poetry, whether or not completely natural, became normal certainly, and was imitated by Juan de Mena as an aesthetic device (and is a part of what is called his deliberate obscurity). Encina, however, uses it sparingly. It will be noted that Virgil's words in this example have a word order that could be translated literally into Spanish, that is to say, word for word, with scarcely any strain on normal Spanish syntax: "La ciudad, que llaman Roma, Melibeo, creía yo—siendo muy bobo—similar a la nuestra." However, one cares to rearrange the Spanish words of this virtually literal translation he need not depart seriously from the pattern used by Virgil. Considering Encina's textual change here, one could write: "La corte, que se dize [que] es del rey, Melibeo, [la] creía—siendo muy bobo yo—similar a nuestro lugar." Given an opportunity for "straight translation," in keeping with the pastoral style he set for himself, Encina chose to complicate his syntax—although not to any startling degree, and with a fine effect. Any number of examples can be found where Encina avoided similar unusual syntactical patterns is Spanish, although it would be natural for him to do so as a result of his working so closely with a Latin text, and, let it not be forgotten, with excellent traditional authority for doing so.

This question of syntax (in poetry a part of the "poetic license") is as curious in Encina's translations of Virgil as is his refraining from utilizing, or developing, what in the Latin poet is a very clear-cut metaphor. Virgil personalizes Rome in this section (haec tantum alias inter caput extulit urbes), but Encina ignores this comparison of a city a head taller than any other and uses instead the abstract concept "te parecerá qual *el plazer con pesares*," a comparison typical (because it is abstract) of Encina and of his period. He retains, however, Virgil's comparison of the cypress with shrubbery.

MELIBOEUS

Et quae tanta fuit Romam tibi causa videndi?

> Y dime qué te movió
> o qué caso tan profundo
> por ventura te acuntió
> que en cariño te metió
> de ver corte y tan gran mundo;
> por tu fe,
> que me digas cómo fue,
> que de pasmo me perhundo.

The obvious difference here between Virgil and Encina can be understood. Melibeo's rather more lengthy response, however, is not carelessly verbose, but is similar to Encina's use of rustic dialogue in his own eclogues: that of intense, repetitive insistence mixed with a natural (and frequently humorous) rustic garrulity and exaggeration (de pasmo me perhundo).

TITYRUS

Libertas, quae sera tamen respexit inertem,
candidior postquam tondenti barba cadebat,
respexit tamen et longo post tempore venit,
postquam nos Amaryllis habet, Galatea reliquit.
namque, fatebor enim, dum me Galatea tenebat,
nec spes libertatis erat, nec cura peculi.
quamvis multa meis exiret victima saeptis,
pinguis et ingratae premeretur caseus urbi,
non umquam gravis aere domum mihi dextra redibat.

Alamiefé, tú te sabe,
que por verme en libertad,
que es lo que más oy se alabe,
y el libre do quiera cabe
y le dan autoridad;
he buscado
cómo me ver libertado
fuera de cautividad.

Mas esta libertad mía
por que yo me emperezava
y mostrava covardía
vino algún poco tardía,
ya que la barva rapava;
y ha traydo
un gasajo tan cumplido
quanto yo lo desseava.

Desque aqueste rey nos tiene
y al otro señor dexamos,
mucho ganado nos viene,
y avn a Dios como conviene
harto diezmo le pagamos;
de buen peso
ya podremos hazer queso
para en villa que vendamos.

> Mas en el otro poder
> libertad no se esperava,
> no gozávamos plazer,
> nada osávamos vender,
> por que no se nos pagava;
> las haziendas
> con trabajos y contiendas
> ninguno no las labrava.

Here Encina departs radically from the concepts of Virgil, although he follows some of Virgil's formal and textual progression. "Liberty," the important element of Tityrus' speech, is given a different emphasis and a different meaning in Encina's version. The very position of the word "libertad" in Encina is not as effective as it is in Virgil; but where in Virgil it means—at least on the immediate literal level of the poem—a freedom from personal abulia, complicated to a certain extent at least by the presence in the shepherd's life of Amaryllis and Galatea, in Encina it takes on a political meaning, and serves not as an answer to Meliboeus' question, but rather as an introduction to five strophes of Encina's interpolation in praise of the King. This interpolation is personal, and in it Encina assumes the role of Tityrus in order to explain, again, why he chose to make this translation in honor of the King.

Encina's personal assumption of the role of Tityrus is seen in a "discrepancy" of his translation, for in Virgil he is an old man who did not become aware of his need for liberty until the clippings from his beard were growing white. Encina follows Virgil's concept of tardy realization, but means here only his having come into manhood, "ya que la barva rapava." (And in the interpolation this is extended to mean until Encina came into his full powers as a poet.) He allows Tityrus to resume his role as an old man after he has delivered the interpolated speech, from which point on Encina follows rather closely the structure and text of the Latin poem. (The interpolation is not entirely unrelated to Virgil textually, however, and this shifting back and forth between semantic and lexical faithfulness is one of the most fascinating aspects of Encina's translation.)

Although the love theme is avoided, Encina follows the text of Virgil in a structural way: "Postquam nos Amaryllis habet" becomes "Desque aqueste rey nos tiene" and the statement "Galatea reliquit [nos]" becomes inverted, "Y *al* otro señor *dexamos*." Encina makes no contrast between the present time and the past, following here—very vaguely—certain leads offered him by Virgil. Note how Tityrus says "nec spes libertatis erat, nec cura peculi." In Encina it becomes, inverted, "mucho ganado nos viene," "ya podremos hazer queso / para en villa que vendamos," which corresponds to the Latin poem *"pinguis* et ingratae premeretur caseus urbi, / non umquam gravis *aere* domum mihi dextra redibat." The Spanish Tytiro does not refer to sacrificial lambs (quamvis multa meis exiret victima saeptis) but he says "y avn a Dios, como conviene, / harto diezmo le pagamos," which implies a healthy profit, and is a reflection on the state of the nation under the Catholic monarchs.

In all of this Encina again makes much greater use of contrast than does Virgil (or perhaps it is better to say a more obvious use); the whole section itself is an inversion of Virgil's concepts, as has been indicated. This complete twisting of Virgil for his own ends corresponds to the fifteenth-century practice of making glosses of other poets' work, and that practice may serve as an explanation of Encina's aesthetics here. Note the unusual, but excellent, parallel between each of the four strophes with their isolated concept formed by the *quebrado* and the last two lines.

After the five strophes sub-titled "Tytiro al rey" Encina returns to Virgil. Encina omits completely Meliboeus' aside to the absent Amaryllis; it is, of course, extraneous to Encina's version (as it is, in a way, to Virgil's). Virgil's Tityrus ignores it, however, more completely than Encina's did; Encina uses some elements of Meliboeus' aside in Tytiro's interpolation, including, of course, the dramatic function of the aside:

MELIBOEUS

Mirabar, quid maesta deos, Amarylli, vocares,
cui pendere sua patereris in arbore poma:
Tityrus hinc aberat. ipsae te, Tityre, pinus,
ipsi te fontes, ipsa haec arbusta vocabant.

> *Tytiro al rey*
> Maravillado me siento,
> o gran rey, qué cosa fuesse

passarme por pensamiento
de tener atrevimiento
que en tus hechos yo scriviesse;
tu justicia
a todos pone codicia
que en loarte nadie cesse.

En tu virtud trasportado
me parava yo a pensar
que estarías enojado
en verme tan descuydado
no escrevir de tu reynar,
y aun asmava
que tu gloria me llamava
que la aprendiesse a contar.

No sé para quién guardavas
que estas églogas trobasse
según las obras obravas;
no sé cómo no mandavas
tal obra se te aplicasse;
¡Juro a mí!
Tytiro no estava aquí
para que su fe mostrasse.

Tytiro vía dezir
árbores, pinos y fuentes;
vía tanto reluzir
la virtud de tu bivir,
que alumbravas tú las gentes;
no sabía
escrevir aunque quería
tus hechos muy ecelentes.

Mas agora ya que entiendo
algún poco deste oficio,
ya que voy más conociendo,
favor te pido serviendo
porque luza mi servicio;
quien te quiere,

> sírvate como supiere,
> que yo servirte codicio.

(A part of Virgil's text is incorporated in the interpolation from the following response; Melibeo, however, has not figured in Encina's long section here.)

TITYRUS

Quid facerem? neque servitio me exire licebat
nec tam praesentes alibi cognoscere divos.
hic illum vidi iuvenem, Meliboee, quotannis
bis senos cui nostra dies altaria fumant.
hic mihi responsum primus dedit ille petenti:
'pascite, ut ante, boves, pueri; submittite tauros.'

> *Tytiro a Melibeo*
> Aquí le vi, Melibeo,
> este rey, siendo zagal;
> y cada mes le ofrendeo,
> le rezo con buen desseo
> que Dios le guarde de mal,
> y que vea
> tanto quanto bien dessea
> su persona muy real.
>
> Si mercedes le pedí
> luego me las otorgó,
> y a otros moços y a mí
> los ganados por aquí
> como de antes nos dexó,
> y las vacas
> dexar hazer alharacas
> con los toros nos mandó.

Ignoring the pagan overtones of the first part of Tityrus' response (in the translation it is not a response) Encina utilizes Virgil's idea of twelve days of offerings, turning it into a Christian monthly observance. Encina's somewhat gratuitous comment on the King's generosity (Si mercedes le pedí, / luego me las otorgó) goes in excess of what Virgil said, but this is a bit of wishful thinking on

Encina's part, since he hoped for great favors from the Court. His translation of "submittite tauros" is fanciful and engaging, a perfect example of the poetic imagination that is seen frequently in this translation. It is in keeping with the characters of rustic shepherds and is unquestionably superior to the more exact modern version in English that is often used today, " 'Lads,' he said, 'let your cattle graze, as you have always done, and put your bulls to stud' " (Rieu, p. 23) (although, to be sure, it was never Rieu's intention to be superior or even poetic). The light touch is always Encina's signature on the best pieces he has produced.

MELIBOEUS

Fortunate senex, ergo tua rura manebunt.
et tibi magna satis, quamvis lapis omnia nudus
limosoque palus obducat pascua iunco.
non insueta graves temptabunt pabula fetas,
nec mala vicini pecoris contagia laedent.
fortunate senex, hic inter flumina nota
et fontes sacros frigus captabis opacum.
hinc tibi, quae semper, vicino ab limite saepes
Hyblaeis apibus florem depasta salicti
saepe levi somnum suadebit inire susurro;
hinc alta sub rupe canet frondator ad auras:
nec tamen interea raucae, tua cura, palumbes,
nec gemere aëria cessabit turtur ab ulmo.

Viejo bien aventurado,
luego tus tierras te tienes,
que te las han ya tornado
aunque son de mal labrado;
ya con ellas te sostienes;
mas yo, triste,
de quantos bienes me viste
no tengo ningunos bienes.

Los pastos no acostumbrados
a las tus reses preñadas,
ni aun a todos tus ganados,
no los ternán destemplados;
ni ternán malas majadas,
ni maldad

de la res de vezindad
terná las tuyas dañadas.

Bien aventurado viejo,
entre estas fuentes y ríos
estarás tú muy sobejo,
tendido sin sobrecejo,
cogendo los ayres fríos;
dormirás
con los sones que oyrás
de las abejas sordíos.

El que cortare la rama,
mientra duermes, cantará,
ni por que estés tú en tu cama
la que paloma se llama
entre tanto dexará
los ronquidos,
ni la tórtola gemidos
desde el olmo cessará.

Encina makes paralled and balanced his translation. It is seen that
Virgil's repetition of "Fortunate senex" does not divide his
"strophe" (call it a segment) into two equal parts, while Encina's
is an equal division. Encina also modified the word order—again
on his own authority, for Virgil used the same word order in both
instances. The contrast between "Viejo bien aventurado" and
"Bien aventurado viejo" is a good one, especially inasmuch as in
Encina, as in Virgil, the first part of the speech refers to Meli-
boeus' preoccupations, notably of his flock, and the second part
is directed to Tityrus' leisurely pleasures. Encina does not omit
any element from Virgil's second half—indeed, he seems to pad
in the line "la que paloma se llama," which of itself is pleassant
to the ear, even onomatopoetic, but in context it is wordy—yet he
manages in two strophes to include the material from eight lines,
whereas in his first two strophes he utilizes five lines of Virgil.
The change Encina made in Virgil's word order (Viejo bien aven-
turado / Bien aventurado viejo) is of some weight in a considera-
tion of the possibility—rather a hesitant supposition in the knowl-
edge of Encina's admiration for Virgil—that Encina attempted to

improve his model. One considers the seriousness of the word *model* in this context.

The onomatopoeia evident in Virgil, especially in "somnum suadebit inire susurro" is nicely transferred by Encina in "los sones que oyrás de las abejas sordíos." Again, pagan mythology is disregarded, and "fontes sacros" and "flumina nota" become simply "estas fuentes y ríos."

Encina's last strophe is somewhat a "problem," not only with its questionable "la que paloma se llama" but particularly in its rhyme, wherein *ráma* seems the rhyme of *cantará*. Thus the "A" rhymes are *rama, cama, llama* and the "B" rhymes are *cantará, dexará, cessará*. It is, of course, as Encina would say, "according to the rules," but it is in contrast to his clearly defined rhymes in the other strophes. In this last strophe, too, there is a parallel construction of *ni-ni*, following Virgil's *nec-nec*, but it is complicated by an irregularity in the parallelism, causing a Subject-Verb-Object to be parallel to a Subject-Object-Verb (paloma-dexará-ronquidos and tórtola-gemidos-cessará). Whether it is deliberate or accidental, or whether it is good or bad poetry, I am not prepared to say. It is interesting, and may have an aesthetic relationship with other examples, some already indicated, of Encina's excellent use of inverted parallelism. Perhaps it is a conscious contrast between *raucae* and *gemere*, in which case attention should also be given to the fact that Encina's last strophe is concerned with sound (as are Virgil's last four lines), and this might explain Encina's curious choice for his contrasting rhymes (ráma-cantará). Encina's gently flowing last two lines have an onomatopoetic relation to Virgil's "turtur ab ulmo," and perhaps the same should be said of the harsher "entre tanto dexará / los ronquidos" and "nec tamen interea raucae."

TITYRUS

Ante leves ergo pascentur in aethere cervi,
et freta destituent nudos in litore pisces,
ante pererratis amborum finibus exsul
aut Ararim Parthus bibet aut Germania Tigrim,
quam nostro illius labatur pectore voltus.

> Y aun por esse tal consuelo
> primero podrán pacer

los ciervos allá en el cielo,
y el mar secarse en el suelo,
y en seco los peces ver,
que yo pueda
de rey que tal fama queda
partirme de le querer.

Primero beverá el parto
en Araris desterrado
y el Germán primero harto
beverá en el río quarto
que fue del Parayso dado,
que es el Tygre,
primero que yo peligre
de aver al rey olvidado.

Encina follows Virgil's rhetorical comparison (*ante...quam*), although he departs from his model, which is *ante...ante...quam*, and makes two parallel comparisons (*ante...quam* and *ante... quam*). There does not seem to be any aesthetic advantage in breaking the strict parallelism made by Virgil in lines one and three (both of which begin with the word "ante"); Encina's *primero-primero* is unbalanced. The advantage that Encina had over Virgil in using his *pie quebrado* to introduce the second component of the *ante...quam* comparison is not followed through to its logical aesthetic development in the second strophe. "Que yo pueda" is forceful, while "que es el Tygre" is not only weak but deceptive in that it appears to be a second element of an *ante...quam* comparison.

As if in compensation for having neglected Virgil's use of mythology, Encina introduces here—to no advantage, I believe—the Christian mythology found in Dante (el río quarto que fue del Parayso dado).

MELIBOEUS

At nos hinc alii sitientes ibimus Afros,
pars Scythiam et rapidum Cretae veniemus Oaxen
et penitus toto divisos orbe Britannos.
en umquam patrios longo post tempore fines,
pauperis et tuguri congestum caespite culmen

post aliquot, mea regna videns, mirabor aristas?
impius haec tam culta novalia miles habebit,
barbarus has segetes? en quo discordia cives
produxit miseros! his nos consevimus agros.
insere nunc, Meliboee, piros, pone ordine vites.
ite meae, quondam felix pecus, ite capellae.
non ego vos posthac viridi proiectus in antro
dumosa pendere procul de rupe videbo;
carmina nulla canam; non me pascente, capellae,
florentem cytisum et salices carpetis amaras.

¡Ay! que nosotros yremos
unos por Lybia sedientos
y otros en Cytia daremos,
y otros a Creta vernemos
por Oaxes con tormentos,
muy perdidos,
por los Britanos partidos
¡ay, qué grandes perdimientos!

Algún tiempo por ventura
ya después de algún agosto
si veré la labradura,
la cabaña y lindadura
de mi padre y mi regosto,
yo bien creo
ser asmado si lo veo,
si por esta tierra abosto.

El hombre de armas feroz
ha de aver estas labranças,
y el estraño con su hoz
mis miesses siegue en su boz;
¡o, qué malas ordenanças
que con guerra
nos echen de nuestra tierra
y de nuestras heredanças!

Habla consigo
¡Ay! qué tiempos son ya tales,
mirad para quien sembramos;
Melibeo, pon parrales,

enxere agora perales,
agora, agora medramos
desdichados;
por nuestros malos pecados
ya nunca cabeça alçamos.

¡Aballa, aballa, ganado!
¡andad, andad, mis cabritas!
que en algún tiempo passádo
siendo yo más prosperado
fuystes vos otras benditas;
no os veré
por las peñas, ni estaré
ya tendido en belloritas.

Ya no cantaré mis trobas,
ni tañeré caramillo,
ni vos otras cabras, bovas,
paceréys ya las escobas
ni las flores del tomillo,
ni veréys
los salzes de que cortéys
con la boca algún ramillo.

The most interesting change that Encina makes in this section of his translation is seen in the second strophe, which corresponds to lines three, four, and five in Virgil. Virgil describes Meliboeus' cabin, its thatched roof and his crop of corn. He refers to this, hyperbolically, as "mea regna." Encina makes this section much more human, much more endowed with feeling as he develops a tripartite construction: *labradura, cabaña, lindadura*. The making of *lindadura* the third element is very effective, an element lacking in Virgil. Furthermore, Encina makes more poignant Melibeo's leave-taking by referring to the shepherd's father, which makes more concrete the concept of home and fatherland:

Si veré la labradura,
la cabaña y lindadura
de mi padre y mi regosto...

Encina's handling of the shepherd's relationship to his animals also seems to be more fully endowed with human feeling than that of the Latin poet's. This is seen, for example, in Encina's felicitous use of "veréys" (for "carpetis," last line), and his avoiding the use of the word "amaras" in this connection, making the "ramillo del salze" a very pleasant thing, and therefore more painful to relinquish.

Virgil's line "*Ite* meae, quondam felix pecus, *ite* capellae" gives Encina authority (if not inspiration) for his effective repetition:

> ¡Aballa, aballa, ganado!
> ¡andad, andad, mis cabritas!...

This is seen in the preceding strophe as well (agora, agora medramos). This aesthetic device is used frequently by Encina, not always to such good advantage, but on the whole very discreetly and effectively.

TITYRUS

Hic tamen hanc mecum poteras requiescere noctem
fronde super viridi: sunt nobis mitia poma,
castaneae molles et pressi copia lactis;
et iam summa procul villarum culmina fumant
maioresque cadunt altis de montibus umbrae.

> Si aquesta noche comigo
> alvergar a tí te plega,
> daréte, mi buen amigo,
> mançanas y pan de trigo,
> y aun miga cocha te cuega,
> y aun castaña;
> vámonos a mi cabaña,
> que ya la noche se allega.

Of note in this final strophe is Encina's addition to the menu of *pan de trigo*, and the touching use of direct address (daréte, mi buen amigo); there is another rejection, here of Virgil's image of shadows falling from the mountaintops (last line). Encina uses instead the much more direct, but not for that reason unpleasant, statement.

* * *

The question of the degree to which Virgil influenced Encina directly in his over-all work, and especially in his dramatic eclogues, cannot be handled succinctly. We have noticed several similarities, and we may attribute these to Virgil's influence, although it may be merely coincidental, or indirect. One noticeable trait, which is very effective in Encina's dialogues (not only in the dramatic eclogues but in several *villancicos*) is apparent also in Virgil: the situation wherein each of the speakers seems to take off on his own line of thought, the other paying little or no attention to what has been said before.

SECOND ECLOGUE

EVEN IF I WERE CAPABLE OF THE TASK, I could not here enter into the question of Virgil's bibliography, nor the problem of his biography, for the obvious reasons of space and my purpose. However readers of other centuries regarded Virgil's Second Eclogue, students of the twentieth century are wont simply to call it Virgil's homosexual eclogue. It is possible that the majority of students of earlier times regarded any homosexual interpretation as something so patently contrary to what may have been considered a literary theme that they, quite naturally, rejected the very possibility. Perhaps the very "reasonable" eighteenth century has the correct answer:

> There is certainly something more intended in this Pastoral than a Description of Friendship or *Platonic* Love; the Sentiments, though chaste, are too warm and passionate for a mere *Platonic* Lover. But there is no Reason to charge *Virgil* on that Account with the unnatural Love of Boys; a Poet may shew his Talent in describing a Passion which he by no Means approves. "The Passion for Boys, Mr. *Bayle* observes, was as common in Pagan Times as that for Girls; a Writer of Eclogues therefore might make his Shepherds talk according to that abominable Passion, as we at present make the Heroes and Heroines of Romances talk, without approving the Passions therein mentioned" (Virgil [London, 1763], pp. 6-7).

Be that as it may, we certainly cannot associate Encina with homosexuality. His vice was Narcissism and he indulges himself to the full in this his Second Eclogue. The *Argumento*:

> Egloga segunda, adonde en persona del autor de aquesta presente obra se introduze un pastor llamado Coridón, el

qual como desseasse cantar y escrevir las hazañas tan dinas
de perdurable memoria del nuestro muy esclarecido rey
don Hernando, no pudiendo callar la grandeza de su fama
que por todo el mundo da bozes y sacude sus alas, con
aquexado pensamiento y continuas vigilias se congoxaba,
temiendo su baxo saber para escrevir de tan alta magestad
no sería favorecido. Mas lidiando con él la fuerça del
aficionado desseo, no pudo resistir la pluma sin entrar en
el gran mar de sus alabanças, para las quales proseguir,
invoca y pide su favor, suplicando no desprecie los ser-
vicios pastoriles y protestando gastar todo el tiempo que
biviere en la cuenta de sus vitorias.

The concept of *Juan del Encina* as a theme in his own works
is perfectly valid, but in the present consideration of his version
of the second eclogue it will not become an important point.
Limiting this study of his translation to aesthetic (or literary)
techniques, the first thing to be noted is that Virgil's poem consists
of a brief introduction followed by a series of songs—lyric
poems—of which Rieu says: "The skill by which each disjointed
utterance is made to lead into the next, each intervening thought
is left unspoken yet revealed, so that the completed chain emerges
as an integral whole, is consummate" p. 129). The possibilities this
framework could have offered to Encina in his "free" (so called
by many people) translation, and especially in view of his own
interests as a poet, is a fascinating thought (but, of course, a poet
only translates something once). Another point of aesthetic interest
lies in the fact that the first eclogue of Virgil is in many ways
a study of contrasts (which Encina handles most admirably) while
in the second eclogue we will note a preponderance of sensual
images based on color (and occasionally smell). (In the first eclogue
the predominant sensual element was auditory.)

1 *Formosum pastor Corydon ardebat Alexim,*
2 *delicias domini, nec, quid speraret, habebat.*
3 *tantum inter densas, umbrosa cacumina, fagos*
4 *adsidue veniebat. ibi haec incondita solus*
5 *montibus et silvis studio iactabat inani.*

> 1 Coridón, siendo pastor
> 2 trobador,
> 3 muy aficionado al rey,

4   espejo de nuestra ley,
5   con amor
6   desseava su favor:
7   mas con mucha covardía
8   no creya
9   de lo poder alcançar;
10 por los montes se salía
11 cada día
12 entre sí solo a pensar.

13 Entre las hayas metido
14 y tendido
15 por las sombras muy señero,
16 y sin ningún compañero,
17 con gemido
18 aquexado y afligido:
19 cercado de pensamiento,
20 con tormento,
21 congoxado de passiones,
22 echava bozes al viento,
23 muy sin tiento
24 diziendo tales razones.

In an attempt to show to what extent Encina is faithful to Virgil in his own composition, each line has been numbered in both poets, and the lexical elements of Virgil's first five lines will be listed in order, with the corresponding elements taken from Encina's first two strophes. Numbers in parentheses refer to the lines of the respective authors.

Virgil		*Encina*	
(1)	Formosum Alexim		———
(1)	pastor Corydon	(1)	Coridón siendo pastor
	———	(1)	trobador
(1)	ardebat	(3)	muy aficionado
	„	(5)	con amor
	„	(21)	congoxado de passiones
	———	(3)	al rey
	———	(4)	espejo de nuestra ley

(2)	delicias domini		———
(2)	nec quid speraret habebat	(6)	desseava su favor
	"	(7)	mucha covardía
	"	(8)	no creya de lo poder alcançar
(3)	inter densas fagos	(13)	Entre las hayas [metido y tendido]
(3)	umbrosa cacumina	(15)	por las sombras
(4)	ibi adsidue veniebat	(10)	se solía cada día
(4)	solus	(12)	entre sí solo
	"	(15)	muy señero
	"	(16)	sin ningún compañero
(5)	iactabat	(22)	echaba bozes (al viento)
	"	(24)	*diziendo* tales razones (See below.)
(5)	montibus	(10)	por los montes

Two concepts from Virgil's lines 4 and 5 have been set aside, since they tend to be blended in Encina's utilization of them:

(4)	haec incondita	(12)	a pensar [studio]
and		(17)	con gemido [incondita]
(5)	inani studio	(18)	aquestado y afligido [incondita]
		(19)	cercado de pensamiento [studio]
		(23)	muy sin tiento [inani]
		(24)	diziendo *tales razones* [haec incondita]

Encina includes in his two strophes every semantic element of Virgil's five lines except three: *1*) formosum Alexim; *2*) delicias domini (although this is corresponded to by "aficionado al rey"); and *3*) silvis (which is adequately implied in Encina's strophes). Encina adds several elements: *1*) trobador; *2*) rey (and the accompanying metaphor "espejo de nuestra ley"); *3*) covardía (not a radical change); and *4*) tormento (again, not radical). None of these seven elements is listed here because of its conceptual value, especially the words "silvis," "covardía," and "tormento," but simply for the lexical value. I believe this comparison between the respective segments of both poems shows as graphically as possible the extent to which Encina did immerse himself in the form and structure of his model. The fact that the two poems in these segments are conceptually distinct is, of course, something else altogether different.

To return for a moment to thematic material, it is obvious that Virgil's poem is on the theme of unrequited love. The nature of Corydon's love (homosexuality aside) finds no place, really, in Encina's vast exploration of the subject. Encina is capable, for example, of chiding most severely a deceitful lover (see the *Bárbola* poems [3]), but he would not consider playing one love against another (see lines 43ff of Virgil). Some comparison might be made with Vitoriano's plea to Flugencia, and the urging of the shepherd's friend in the *villancico* "Dacá, baylemos, Carillo". The theme of Encina's version of this eclogue is a combination of two themes that are, perhaps, even more dynamic than his love theme: politics (patriotism) and writing. It is, indeed, the prime

---

[3] Encina wrote a very direct, in many ways painful, poem on the subject of scorned love; the woman is identified through the acrostic "BARBOLA BARBOLA" which initiates each strophe. There are other poems, one excellent example in his rustic poetry, on the same theme; and one may group them together as the "Bárbola" poems. In this poem, "Juan del Enzina a su amiga por que se desposó" (fo. [77]), we see the following harsh attack of a psychological nature, so very different from the sweet pain of other rejected lovers (Encina also) of the period:

> quando estéys más descuydada
> sin pensamiento de enojos
> lloraréys con vuestros ojos
> y seréys muy mal tratada...
>
> ... ...
> Luego luego no ay cuydados,
> mas a la larga después,
> quanto más va peor es
> la vida de los casados...
>
> ... ...
> Andando el tiempo y edad
> vos diréys ¡ay, ay, mezquina!
> que el triste Juan del Enzina
> bien me dixo la verdad...

example of what Andrews calls "Prometheus in Search of Prestige." [4]

As has been implied, if not always indicated, throughout this present study of his aesthetics, Encina was occasionally careless or clumsy in his handling of words, but he was very rarely, if ever, thoughtless in choosing them. In the context that Andrews studies Encina, the word "trobador" (line 2 of the translation) is an isolated and therefore outstanding word (in *pie quebrado*), and Andrews might also have mentioned the aesthetic significance of this word, which is the keynote of the whole translation. "Trobador" does not mean "poeta." Remember Chapter III of the *Arte de poesía*, "De la diferencia que ay entre poeta y trobador." "Trobador," then, is a very humble word, and one, moreover, that stands out, as I have mentioned. It is not an example of affected modesty so much as it is Encina's attempt to recreate the despondency of Corydon (nec quid speraret habebat)—his feeling of inadequacy. Also, remember Encina's explanation in the *Arte de poesía* of the meaning of *trobar*: to seek. So, for Encina, "trobador" is a tremendously "beseeching" word. In addition to a framework, and several accurately transcribed descriptions, Encina also copies here the *feeling* that Virgil created of a rejected lover. Juan del Encina, as much as Corydon, is abject, beseeching and grovelling. It is hoped that this attitude of both poets will be noticed throughout the following comparison; further mention of it will not be made here.

An example of the way in which Encina utilizes the framework, and more, the lexicon of Virgil, is seen in the correspondences given for the phrases "haec incondita" and "inani studio." *Studio* leads Encina to use the expressions "se salía cada día entre sí solo a *pensar*" and "cercado de *pensamiento*" (as does also the word "incondita"). However, these elements, so called, are not parallel in the two writers. One might say that they are used in a positive sense in Encina and in a negative sense in Virgil.

'O crudelis Alexi, nihil mea carmina curas?
nil nostri miserere? mori me denique coges.

---

[4] J. Richard Andrews, *Juan del Encina: Prometheus in Search of Prestige,* University of California Publications in Modern Philology, LIII (Berkeley and Los Angeles, 1959), pp. 44-47.

O rey de reyes primor,
y señor
de las tierras y los mares,
no curas de mis cantares
ni has dolor
de aqueste tu servidor:
déxasme triste morir
y sufrir
por no me favorecer
para te aver de servir
y escrevir
algo de tu merecer.

Encina omits the harsh adjective "crudelis," admitting nonetheless the King's lack of pity (miserere/dolor) and allowing him to be the cause of the poet's death. The expected death of lovers was so common in fifteenth-century and in Encina's poetry that it had lost its impact as an image (especially, I should think, when it is "triste" and when it is ineffectually coupled as it is here with "sufrir"). Virgil is simpler.

nunc etiam pecudes umbras et frigora captant,
nunc virides etiam occultant spineta lacertos,
Thestylis et rapido fessis messoribus aestu
alia serpullumque herbas contundit olentes.

Ora en estos temporales
tan mortales
los ganados con calores
buscan sombras y frescores
muy frescales
y los lagartos çarçales:
y agora en aqueste estío
tan crudío
Testilis coge las rosas
por dar al segador frío
y amorío
y otras yervas olorosas.

Touch and smell are included in these verses. The immense depiction here is all Virgil's, although Encina may deserve credit for his condensation, even though he may merit none for "frescores muy frescales." (This manner of emphasis in Encina, and the fifteenth century, is one not at all easy to judge. I think we might call it a "dangerous" aesthetic device—that is to say, one that is less apt to work than the poet hopes. But there is, indeed, some "freshness" in the use of frescores / frescales, part of which may be due to the simple technique of using the two similar words in different lines. Many examples of this manner are found in Encina's work.) In spite of the fact that Encina uses only one strophe for four lines we note both an addition and a repetition. "Frescores muy frescales" is repetitive, and one cannot cease to wonder at the mystery of language that allows a poet, such as Encina, to have words to spare in such limited space, especially when he adds the concept "temporales tan *mortales*," which demands an explanation in this context.

Menéndez y Pelayo has stated, in connection with Encina's translation of Virgil, that the Spaniard was engaging in parody. ("Interpretó libremente a Virgilio con un desenfado que ya degenera en irreverencia y parodia..." *Antología*, V, 179). [5] This point of view was rejected entirely by Andrews (p. 34 ff.), who studied this second eclogue particularly, and who also referred to the derogatory interpretation made by Mayáns earlier. There is a sort of "parody" here, although it is my belief that the word always has the connotation of malicious intent. In this strophe of Encina is, perhaps, the best example of how one may apply the term to his version (although there is not the slightest temptation to suspect mockery or deprecation on Encina's part, here or elsewhere in the translations). Here he changes garlic into roses. (It might be interesting, also, to consider Encina's choice of "olorosas" for "olentes." Parody is a consideration in Encina's work, notably in *Plácida y Vitoriano*, where it is used seriously, and (rarely) when he uses hyperbaton in a very light poem for humorous intent. [6]

---

[5] Marcelino Menéndez Pelayo, *Antología de poetas líricos castellanos*, V (Buenos Aires, 1952), p. 179.

[6] An example is a gently self-mocking description of how his coat was stolen:

> Por que, señor, sé de cierto
> que de mi plazer os plaze,
> *mi capa saber os haze*
> como se fue con un tuerto...   (fo. [56])

at mecum raucis, tua dum vestigia lustro,
sole sub ardenti resonant arbusta cicadis.

> Mas yo triste, sin consuelo,
> con recelo,
> en tí mi memoria puesta,
> ándome toda la siesta
> por mi duelo
> y aun de noche me desvelo:
> por que favor no posseo
> yo rodeo
> las arboledas y parras,
> no veo lo que desseo;
> antes veo
> comigo cantar cigarras.

At this point of the two poems we enter a section wherein Encina begins to omit Virgil and add his own ideas and statements. The sections just quoted are fairly correspondent, although it should be noted that Encina does not here use the perhaps unpleasant idea of "sub sole ardenti," substituting instead the concept of "toda la siesta"; nor can Encina say, in directing himself to the King, that he is "following [in]his footsteps." Therefore he adds his obvious contrast—that of night and day: "toda la siesta" and "de noche me desvelo." The spirit, even the lexicon, of Encina's strophe does not correspond entirely to the two lines quoted above, but does so in relation to several others of Virgil's lines in this section of the poem.

Again, reference to Amaryllis is omitted, and thus the lines

nonne fuit satius, tristes Amaryllidis iras
atque superba pati fastidia? nonne Menalcan,

have no direct counterpart in Encina. Instead, Encina adds a personal plea:

> ¿Piensas quiçá por ventura
> la escritura
> de los cantos pastoriles,
> aunque en palabras más viles
> se figura,

que no requiere cordura?
aunque tu muy gran poder
deva ser
más loado, y más mereces,
doblarás con tu querer
mi saber
si tú, rey, me favoreces.

Encina picks up in the following strophe Virgil's "narrative," which has been broken here after the word "Menalcan." The following lines of Virgil are a part of the sequence interrupted above (and in which "rey" is equivalent to "Menalcan" in a lexical sense and to "Alexis" and "Amaryllidis" in a conceptual sense):

quamvis ille niger, quamvis tu candidus esses?
o formose puer, nimium ne crede colori:

¡O gran rey de gran potencia
y prudencia,
por la color no te creas!
Aunque ser pastor me veas,
tu ecelencia
me dará gran eloquencia:
por ser rústico zagal
y assí tal
de tí desechado estoy;
no hazes de mí caudal;
por mi mal
nunca preguntas quién soy.

Encina passes over completely one line of Virgil that is in every way "safe" for what he wants to say to the King, and which is also a line that could be used to good advantage in his translation:

alba ligustra cadunt, vaccinia nigra leguntur.

(We are not sure, of course, that this line was in "Encina's Virgil.") The following line in Virgil:

despectus tibi sum nec, qui sim, quaeris, Alexi,

is, however, included in Encina (por mi mal / nunca preguntas quién soy.) There is no apparent explanation why Encina should choose to ignore the line, which is (its poetic virtues aside) so much in keeping with his love of poetic contrast. This omission, however, must be noted, more so than some others which are understandable. The rest of the second eclogue is followed closely by Encina, with relatively slight textual variations (although the conceptual differences are sometimes great, of course).

quam dives pecoris, nivei quam lactis abundans:
mille meae Siculis errant in montibus agnae;
lac mihi non aestate novum, non frigore defit.
canto, quae solitus, si quando armenta vocabat,
Amphion Dircaeus in Actaeo Aracyntho.

> ¡Cuán rico soy de ganado
> y abastado
> de leche en todo tempero!
> mil borregas he de apero,
> bien chapado,
> y todas a tu mandado:
> téngote mucha afición,
> con razón:
> rey sobre todos los reyes,
> canto la mesma canción
> que Anfión
> quando llamava sus greyes.

As was noted above, Encina avoided a repetition of the concept (and lexicon) of summer heat. A similar avoidance is to be noted here: Virgil uses (line 21 of his poem) the word "aestate," a repetition of "aestu" (line 10). Encina does not repeat "estío" or a variant, a notable point, inasmuch as Encina can be accused of duplicating his lexicon to too great an extent in others of his works. It will be noted also that he avoids—one might say judiciously—the accumulation of names (amphion Dircaeus in Actaeo Aracyntho), which he does not avoid on other occasions, as for example when in the "Triunfo de fama" (which was written upon his completion of this translation) he writes:

> Propercio, Mevanio, con Albio, Tibulo,
> y Galo, Cornelio, Syleta y Catulo.

Again it must be noted that Encina avoids the opportunity to make a strong visual image of the word "white," Virgil saying "nivei lactis," Encina limiting himself to "leche." Such restraint, if, indeed, restraint is quite the right word, is puzzling. We notice how Encina will elaborate on a word or two of Virgil, as in the above strophe, where Virgil's "mille agnae" becomes "Mil borregas he de apero, bien chapado." And while it is very easy to understand why Encina says what he does say in the following strophe, it is not at all easy to understand why he avoids the very concrete possibilities of the mirror image presented by Virgil.

nec sum adeo informis: nuper me in litore vidi,
cum placidum ventis staret mare; non ego Daphnim
iudice te metuam, si numquam fallit imago.

> Ni yo soy tan bovo, ahé,
> que no sé
> conocer menguas y sobras,
> que no ha mucho que en mis obras
> me agrade,
> sino me cegó la fe:
> mas a tí para alabarte,
> sin errarte,
> más y más saber deviera;
> mas no cessaré loarte
> de mi parte
> aunque me juzgue qualquiera.

To a certain extent, although not particularly in the last strophe quoted, Encina's omissions and elaborations cause us, in a close comparison of his version with its source, to pay closer attention than we might under ordinary circumstances to the care with which he has been constructing his verses. In his translations of Virgil Encina is writing extremely well—with very few of the unpleasant lapses noticeable in other works of his. One notices the fluidity of each line and the cohesion of rhyme within the strophe. (Note the "long" grammatical sequences of the strophes in this eclogue especially.) In the last strophe quoted, one may note his excellently employed interjection "ahé"—which makes perfect the rhythm as it progresses in the second line "que no sé."

o tantum libeat mecum tibi sordida rura
atque humiles habitare casas et figere cervos
haedorumque gregem viridi compellere hibisco!
mecum una in silvis imitabere Pana canendo.

> Plega a Dios que en nuestra aldea
> yo te vea
> ver las obras de tus siervos
> y andar a caça de ciervos,
> por que sea
> como mi gana dessea:
> mira que Pan inventó
> y ordenó
> los albogues tañedores
> y ovejas apacentó
> y él tomó la guarda de los pastores.

Pan primum calamos cera coniugere plures
instituit, Pan curat oves oviumque magistros.
nec te paeniteat calamo trivisse labellum:
haec eadem ut sciret, quid non faciebat Amyntas?

> No te deve de pesar
> semejar
> al nuestro Pan en cantares;
> por las silvas y lugares,
> sin dudar,
> me dexa de tí cantar:
> no recibas por enojo
> ni cordojo
> tocar nuestro caramillo,
> que Amintas con gran antojo
> abre el ojo
> por semejar pastorcillo.

Of interest in these two strophes is the way in which Encina avoids the intimacy of approach that Virgil's shepherd uses. Encina does not offer to instruct the King in the art of singing (although it must not be forgotten that he did not hesitate to instruct the Prince in the Art of Poetry). Unlike Corydon's offer to Alexis, Encina implies that the King is already versed in all the arts, rustic or otherwise; Encina twists the text slightly in order to explain to the King not how Pan was generous nor Amyntas willing, but rather how the King would not demean himself should he choose to play their roles. The King will hunt, to be sure, but he will not drive the herd of goats! (That this is equally applicable to Encina himself is a point that by this time we can scarcely miss.) Notice in Encina's first strophe here how the second half changes tense and provides a series of "agudo" endings.

The following strophes follow almost exactly the original, omitting only the reference to Thestylis.

est mihi disparibus septem compacta cicutis
fistula, Damoetas dono mihi quam dedit olim
et dixit moriens "te nunc habet ista secundum."
dixit Damoetas, invidit stultus Amyntas.
praeterea duo, nec tuta mihi valle reperti,
capreoli, sparsis etiam nunc pellibus albo;
bina die siccant ovis ubera; quos tibi servo.
iam pridem a me illos abducere Thestylis orat;
et faciet, quoniam sordent tibi munera nostra.

Tengo una flauta muy buena
que bien suena,
de siete diversas bozes
para que tú della gozes;
muy sin pena
tañe qualquier cantilena:
Dametas quando murió
me la dió
por que mucho me quería,
y aun Amintas, que lo vió,
recibió
gran embidia en demasía.

Dos cabritos buenos he
que apañé
en no muy seguro valle;
manchados y de buen talle

los hallé;
con ellos te serviré:
nunca cessan de mamar
y engordar;
que ya por ellos me ruegan,
quiçá los avré de dar
y endonar
si tus favores me niegan.

The exactness with which Encina translates Virgil here is surprising (I am not referring to the condensation, although that is something curious), for he, like Corydon, threatens the King (quiçá los avré de dar...si tus favores me niegan; et faciet, quoniam sordent tibi munera nostra). Judging by his handling of other material in this second eclogue, one would have expected a different "translation."

* * *

Virgil's poem consists of 74 lines and Encina's of 23 strophes. The first 44 lines of Virgil correspond to the first 13 strophes of Encina (including the additions). Encina's final ten strophes follow Virgil's final 30 lines. In particular it should be noted that strophes 14 to 20 correspond to lines 45 to 62, while strophes 21 to 23 correspond to lines 63-74. It is difficult to pair lines of Virgil with strophes of Encina in this latter half of the poem. The way Encina moves from one line to a relatively distant one might lead one to suspect that his method of translation (here at least) was to work without a text but through memory. Nonetheless, the similarity of details in the two poems (given, always, Encina's twisting of them) indicates otherwise. The following comparisons are among the loveliest, both in Virgil and in Encina:

huc ades, o formose puer: tibi lilia plenis
ecce ferunt Nymphae calathis, tibi candida Nais,
pallentes violas et summa papavera carpens,
narcissum et florem iungit bene olentis anethi;
tum casia atque aliis intexens suavibus herbis
mollia luteola pingit vaccinia caltha.
ipse ego cana legam tenera lanugine mala
castaneasque nuces, mea quas Amaryllis amabat;

addam cerea pruna: honos erit huic quoque pomo;
et vos, o lauri, carpam et te, proxima myrte,
sic positae quoniam suaves miscetis odores.

> Ven agora, rey precioso,
> poderoso,
> y a mis obras da favores;
> las Ninfas lirios y flores
> con reposo
> te traen, o rey gracioso:
> violetas amarillas
> y pardillas,
> Náyade la más luziente,
> dormideras maravillas
> de rodillas
> te presenta por presente.

The strophe demands attention for several reasons, especially the unusual hyperbaton of the second half which forces our attention on the exquisite "dormideras maravillas," a line worthy of Góngora. The strophe is complicated and elaborated for a purpose, however. Here Encina is speaking about his works, and in this way draws attention in a striking manner to his mastery as a poet. It is different from the rest of the poem, and very unlike almost all of his other poetry. It is not only extremely contrived, but it embodies some philological complexities that can only be considered a kind of linguistic game reserved for insiders. It is particularly lovely, and Encina must have been proud of his poetical coup.

Encina uses here very unusual hyperbaton, twice in the same strophe. (The colon [:] is Encina's own punctuation and one that usually separates the strophe into two thought groups. See his *Arte de poesía castellana*, Ch. V.) "Las ninfas te traen lirios y flores" is the normal syntax of the first half (*verso* in Encina's terminology). The second *verso* must be read on one level as "La más luziente Náyade te presenta violetas [que son] dormideras maravillas," and on another as "Náyade te presenta violetas, dormideras [y] maravillas." The two *versos* form a contrast, with a Subject-Object-Verb (plus vocative) forming a parallel with an Object-Subject-Verb (plus Object in apposition immediately after the Subject), which is a poetical practice of Encina's on other occasions.

Encina is very careful of parallelism as a rhetorical device, which explains, I believe, his occasional use of the inverted parallelism. See, for example, the first eclogue ("Fortunate senex," l. 46 ff.), where I consider this aspect. In the first eclogue it may be questioned whether or not this is a deliberately complicated aesthetic device; but in the "flower strophe" under consideration, there is no question: Encina is speaking of his writing, and there is really no theme in all his work handled so adamantly. "A mis obras da favores," he is saying, and he would ensnare us in his trap, compelling us to give serious consideration to his talents as a writer.

Unlike the difficult poetry of many another writer, however, the level of difficulty and complication is not an immediate one. Whether or not one appreciates or even recognizes all the subtleties, the meaning of the strophe, on a literal level, is perfectly clear: "Nymph and Naiad give you flowers (*lirios, violetas, dormideras, maravillas*)." The beautiful line "dormideras maravillas" has a double meaning not at all difficult to perceive; i.e., 'poppies, maravillas [flowers]' as well as 'sleeping wonders.' Had Encina wished to clarify the reading of the line as a bipartite series, he could have supplied the slash [/], which he uses on other occasions—and in strophes much less personally important to him. (Incidentally, this sort of pun in poetry soon became impossible, as books printed in Italic type very early incorporated the modern comma. Encina's 1496 *Cancionero* was in Gothic, as were most incunabula of Salamanca, including Nebrija's works.) See, for example, Encina's use of a "comma":

tu valer / aver / saber
tu poder / querer / tener (fo. 79ᵛ)

Since we are dealing here not only with a highly elaborated strophe concerning his talents as an artist, but with a translation as well, we note that Encina translates 'pallentes violas' as 'violetas amarillas / y pardillas.' 'Amarillas,' according to its usage at the time and its etymology (cf. Joan Corominas, *DCEC*, art. 'amarillo'), corresponds exactly to 'pallentes.' 'Pardillas,' as we know, means 'grey,' 'dusky grey,' 'greyish brown,' 'brownish,' etc., and seems to mean so in other poems of Encina (e.g., when he describes the clothing of rustics). But how very peculiar it is to see 'pardillas' as a description of a violet. We must disregard the two likeliest explanations, that it is a bit of carelessness or that it is a bit of liberty, because the strophe itself is obviously conceived as one of great importance to Encina (suffice it to say that he was totally serious—as was Virgil—when he asked the King to recognize him).

Encina is playing in this strophe on a linguistic-philological level beyond that of the ordinary reader (including the King and the Queen), but on a level that could possibly be meant to titillate—or even tease—his mentor Nebrija and / or some others of whatever particular academic-poetic circle Encina belonged to. Very curiously—and to the confusion, also, of Corominas—Nebrija lists in his Spanish-Latin Lexicon as a translation of Spanish 'pardo' Latin 'venetus.' There seems to be no question that 'venetus' means some shade of blue (this is true both in Latin and in its later vulgar forms). (Palencia, in his *Universal vocabulario* does not list 'venetus.' St. Isidore in his *Etymologies* lists it several times, as a blue color.) Now Encina very well could have changed the translation from 'pale violets' to 'pale and *blue* violets' without affecting radically the context, or the lexicon (nor changing the *colors* presents in Virgil). No one—or hardly anyone— could have recognized what Encina was doing here. One would suspect that 'pardillas' in this instance was used as a variation of 'pallentes' (perhaps not very satisfactorily). But when Encina says 'violetas pardillas' he means 'blue violets'; and he his playing some kind of philological game, and one which I suspect depends on Nebrija's translation of 'pardo' as 'venetus.'

The names of colors, as is well-known, present curious philological problems, as do the names of plants and flowers. In this strophe we have a problem of each kind. 'Maravilla' is a flower possessing at least fifteen (and doubtless many more) different forms. Many of them are from the New World, as in Góngora's famous 'maravilla,' which he used ("Aprended, flores, en mí") in the same pun of "flower / marvellous thing" that Encina did.

'Maravilla' is an addition to the poem's flowers, just as 'pardilla' is an addition to the colors, for it does not appear in Virgil's list; Encina also adds 'rosa' in the following strophe, calling it "rosa de aquel narciso color," which corresponds to Virgil's 'narcissum.' He also adds, among the plants of the succeeding strophes, the 'encinal'; but the poetic purpose of that is easy to see. Let us at least question if the addition of 'pardillas' and 'maravillas' serves a poetic function other than that of merely two nice rhymes of 'amarillas.' In his translations Encina is very faithful to the lexicon and the semantics of Virgil, contrary to what has often been said, and additions and deletions in the translations are never haphazard, and should be studied with particular care. There is no question, I should think, of the pun 'maravilla-flower / marvellous things,' since the flowers here represent his poems ("A mis obras da favores"). Thus, by contact, 'dormideras' displays its two meanings of 'sleeping' and 'poppies.' In the position it has here—not only in the emphatic one of *pie quebrado*, but as an appositive—we read it as modifying the noun ('sleeping wonder'), or as one of a bipartite series, ('poppies and *maravilla-*flowers'). The concept of 'dormant wonders' [his work] is in accord with his own evaluation elsewhere of the difficulty of some of his poems.

The logical step for the curious investigator is to decide exactly what kind of flower Encina had in mind when he added 'maravilla' to Virgil's list. Many a large and weighty volume dedicated to the flora of Europe, Spain, and other regions, led me to believe that the 'maravilla' was, then as now, the common Spanish name of the calendula, or marygold. Dr. Laguna (in the only reference I have found relatively contemporary to Encina) lists a blue *maravilla*, from Andalusia, which I do not find so listed in any of the nineteenth or twentieth century encyclopedias of flora I have consulted). Encina, however, uses the 'maravilla' on another occasion, along with 'amarillas,' again in a double pun: "Demuestran las maravillas / las que Dios hizo en hazeros, / su color ser amarillas, / mis presiones sin manzillas...(fo. 83). ('Amarilla' meaning not only 'pale' [pallentes violas], and 'pale yellow,' but also 'bitter.') [7]

---

[7] Some other examples of these words from the fifteenth century: in Encina's *Cancionero,* from the "Disparates" (and therefore not really helpful): "y salieron las arañas / con sus ropas de amarillo," (fo. 58); from the sixth Virgilian Eclogue, "Con estos dos moçalvillos / temerosos y amarillos...," (fo. 41); and from the first Virgilian Eclogue, "ando triste y

There is one reference to a 'maravilla' that I find intriguing in this connection. In several dictionaries of Galician it is listed as "Hierba oficinal, cuyas flores pajizas se renuevan todos los meses, de donde viene la frase; *Como a frol da maravilla: cátama morta, cátama viva.* También se llama *frol de todo o ano.*" [8] If Encina's 'maravilla" were the Galician one, then one could perceive an even more involved pun, resolved very roughly in English as "a sleeping neversleep." *Autoridades* lists 'maravilla': "La flor de la maravilla, cátala viva. Phrase con que se dá à entender la poca consistencia y firmeza de alguna cosa." Such an interpretation of the popular *refrán* is inevitable if one thinks of Góngora's 'maravilla'; but if the original flower of the *refrán* were the one just indicated in the Galician dictionaries, an entirely different interpretation might be made. It would serve as an example of the relatively sudden semantic reversals one is apt to find in the names of plants and colors.

This last consideration of 'maravilla' is one I offer with many reservations, naturally; but the idea that Encina would not engage in such linguistic chicanery most definitely is not one of them.

---

amarillo," (fo. 33). Also from the fifteenth-century Don Juan Manuel, in Menéndez y Pelayo, *Antología...*, III, 291, the *romance* "Gritando va el caballero":

> De una madera amarilla
> Que llaman desesperar,
> Paredes de canto negro
> ... ...
> El suelo hizo de plomo
> Porque es pardillo metal...

In the *villancico* "Tan buen ganadico," cited by Menéndez y Pelayo as anonymous (*Antología*, III, 421), but attributed to Encina (it is doubtless his) in the *Cancionero Musical de los Siglos XV y XVI*:

> Vestí mi ganado
> de azul y pardillo,
> porque he sospechado
> que pasce otro exido.

[8] Eladio Rodríguez González, *Diccionario enciclopédico gallego-castellano,* 3 vols. (Vigo, 1958-1961). See also Juan Cuveiro Piñol, *Diccionario Gallego* (Barcelona, 1876), "maravilla—planta. V. *Herba do podador.* Tienen la propiedad sus flores, que son amarillas, de renovarse todos los meses en la planta y por eso se dice 'flor de la maravilla cátala muerta cátala viva.' "

Para tí coge la rosa
muy hermosa
de aquel narciso color,
y el eneldo con su flor
olorosa,
y cassia muy virtuosa:
siempre piensa en contentarte
y llevarte
flores blandas y alagüeras:
nunca cessa de ayuntarte
y buscarte
yervas de dos mil maneras.

Yo tan bien con una gana
muy ufana
para tu real corona
cogeré por mi persona
la mançana
con su flor muy loçana:
cogeré del castañal,
y enzinal
las bellotas y castañas,
pues tu fama es immortal,
triunfal,
con vitorias muy estrañas.

These two strophes are much less interesting; one dislikes the vague "*aquel* narciso color" (and even "narciso *color*"), "yervas *de dos mil maneras*," "vitorias muy *estrañas*." Likewise (this construction may interest some readers) "cogeré del *castañal* y enzinal las bellotas y *castañas*," although one cannot but smile appreciatively at our poet's gratuitous inclusion here of the *enzinal*.

Y otras frutas más y más
de mí avrás
dexándonos Dios bivir;
si con gana recebir
las querrás
muy gran merced les harás:
tan bien os he de cortar

> y podar,
> o laureles y arrayhanes,
> por que siempre soléys dar
> y mezclar
> olores dulces, galanes.

The strophe is of interest mostly for the not altogether rare use of *encabalgamiento* which produces the strange line "las querrás." (*Encabalgamiento* in Encina has not been discussed, but it is not very rare, although usually it is not so abrupt. Its use in the fifteenth century is of interest; observe it in Jorge Manrique's *Coplas*.) The idea of "olores *dulces, galanes*" is intriguing.

rusticus es, Corydon; nec munera curat Alexis,
nec, si muneribus certes, concedat Iollas.
heu, heu, quid volui misero mihi? floribus Austrum
perditus et liquidis immisi fontibus apros.
quem fugis, ah, demens? habitarunt di quoque silvas
Dardaniusque Paris. Pallas, quas condidit arces,
ipsa colat: nobis placeant ante omnia silvae.

> *Habla consigo*
> No cura el rey de tu don,
> Coridón,
> que eres rústico aldeano;
> otro avrá más cortesano
> de fación
> de quien haga más mención:
> ¡ay, mezquino! ¡en qué cuydado
> tan penado
> he puesto mi pensamiento!
> mal he sido aconsejado;
> lazerado,
> yo mesmo busqué tormento.
>
> ¿A quién huyes? ¿con qué guerras
> te destierras?
> Encubre, encubre tus faltas,
> y no escrivas cosas altas,
> que lo yerras,
> ni huyas de por las sierras:

que los dioses no huyeron,
antes fueron
de las silvas moradores;
los que a Paris conocieron
me dixeron
que bivió con labradores.

Pálas, que torres labró
y fundó,
more en las torres pomposas
y escriva las grandes cosas,
quien buscó
gran saber y lo alcançó:
mas nosotros los villanos
rusticanos
montes y silvas busquemos;
pongamos en hechos llanos
nuestras manos,
de los grandes no curemos.

Encina follows here rather closely his model. Several of Encina's poems, both in his *Cancionero* and in the *Cancionero Musical* (as well as his own actions) correspond to this idea of "exile" or "separation."

One may ask why Encina does not take advantage here of Virgil's lead in the ejaculation "heu, heu." Encina has done it before. The answer is simple, but not without importance. Here Encina is speaking in his "own" language, and such outbursts (even in Virgil) are rustic. Encina may refer to himself as a "villano rusticano," but he, *personally*, refrains from speaking like one here.

The following strophes are good. Virgil is rich in imagery and Encina follows it. They require little comment.

torva leaena lupum sequitur, lupus ipse capellam,
florentem cytisum sequitur lasciva capella,
te Corydon, o Alexi: trahit sua quemque voluptas.

La leona sigue al lobo
por el robo,
y el lobo sigue a la cabra

por que la come y la labra
de su adobo;
la cabra al florido escobo;
y a tí, rey muy virtuoso,
yo cuydoso
por escrivir tus arreos,
que en este mundo penoso
sin reposo
son diversos los desseos.

aspice, aratra iugo referunt suspensa iuvenci,
et sol crescentes decedens duplicat umbras:
me tamen urit amor; quis enim modus adsit amori?
ah, Corydon, Corydon, quae te dementia cepit?

Mira que sufren colgados
los arados,
los toros el tiempo andando,
y el sol se va derrocando;
mis cuydados
no los puedo ver domados:
en mi penada passión
y afición
¿qué modo terné, mezquino?
¡ay, Coridón, Coridón,
buen garçón,
qué locura que te vino!

semiputata tibi frondosa vitis in ulmo est.
quin tu aliquid saltem potius, quorum indiget usus,
viminibus mollique paras detexere iunco?
invenies alium, si te hic fastidit, Alexim.'

Fin
Agora ya començada
y enlazada
mi gana en tan gran dezir,
cúmpleme de proseguir
la jornada
y buscar fuerça esforçada:
haré quanto más pudiere

> y supiere,
> mostraré mi buena fe;
> si con esto no cumpliere,
> ni sirviere,
> otro modo buscaré.

In the last lines of his version, Encina makes another interesting switch. (One might like to call them "tropes of translation.") Virgil's Corydon says that perhaps he will find another person to love; Encina says that he will find another way to praise the King.

The penultimate strophe should be singled out as an example of Encina at his best, especially the line "y el sol se va derrocando." (Antonio Machado wrote "El sol va declinando.") Virgil's corresponding line is also especially beautiful: "et sol crescentes decedens duplicat umbras." It is both pleasant and surprising to realize that a "minor" Spanish poet of the fifteenth century can be so good.

FOURTH ECLOGUE

IT IS ALMOST INEVITABLE TO WRITE ABOUT THE FOURTH ECLOGUE. "No short poem in any language has been so much discussed as the Fourth Eclogue," says Rieu (p. 136). I have heard that a Virgilian bibliography published some twenty-five years ago lists almost 4,000 items for this eclogue alone.

It stands out in Encina's translations because he used for it the *verso de arte mayor*. It is not an example of his best poetry, by any means, but it is revealing of his aesthetics. I will allow myself some liberties in my discussion of this poem and try to approach some aspects of Encina's aesthetical processes, aspirations and limitations that I have not touched on before. I will not comment much on the *arte mayor*, but it must be seen (or heard) in every line. It must be compared, line for line, and sound for sound, with those lines of Virgil which, I believe, Encina thought he was duplicating with this line.

The *argumento*, with some emphasis supplied:

> En alabança y loor de los muy vitoriosos y cristianíssimos príncipes Don Hernando y Doña Ysabel, reyes naturales y señores nuestros. Aplicada al nacimiento bienaventurado del nuestro muy esclarecido príncipe Don Juan su hijo, adonde manifiestamente parece Sibila profetizar dellos; *y Virgilio aver sentido de aqueste tan alto nacimiento,* pues que después dél en nuestros tiempos avemos gozado de tan crecidas vitorias y triunfos y vemos la justicia ser no menos poderosa en el mayor que en el menor. Ya los menores no saben qué cosa es temer las sin razones y demasías que en otro tiempo los mayores les hazían; ya con la santa inquisición han acendrado nuestra fe y cada día la van más esclareciendo. Ya no se sabe en sus señoríos y reynos qué cosa sean judíos; ya los

ypócritas son conocidos y cada uno es tratado según
bive. Las virtudes son por su providencia beniníssima-
mente favorecidas y los vicios severíssimamente castiga-
dos. Ya Dios nos da los tiempos a su causa como nosotros
los desseamos.

Sicelides Musae, paulo maiora canamus.
non omnes arbusta iuvant humilesque myricae;

> Musas de Sicilia, dexemos pastores,
> alcemos las velas del nuestro dezir,
> razón nos combida aver de escrevir
> misterios más altos de cosas mayores:
> ni a todos agradan los grandes primores,
> ni a todos tampoco las cosas palpables;
> cantemos estilo notable a notables
> y suene el menor allá con menores.

si canimus silvas, silvae sint consule dignae.
Ultima Cumaei venit iam carminis aetas;
magnus ab integro saeclorum nascitur ordo.
iam redit et Virgo, redeunt Saturnia regna;
iam nova progenies caelo demittitur alto.

> Si silvas cantamos, las silvas merecen
> de rey tan notable gozarse y dar gloria,
> pues reyna tal rey de tanta vitoria
> los grandes triunfos a él se enderecen:
> los bienes comiençan, los males fenecen,
> según que Sibila lo canta y lo reza,
> gran orden comiença en su realeza,
> los reynos saturnios en él rebivecen.
>
> La mesma justicia con él ha venido,
> del cielo nos vino tal generación;
> o Virgen María, tú da perfeción
> al príncipe nuestro, Don Juan ya nacido:
> por tí le veamos muy favorecido,
> pues reyna en la tierra tan cristiano rey,
> tal reyna, tan santa luz de nuestra ley,
> que en todas sus obras es Dios muy servido.

The first question that may occur to one reading Encina's translation for the first time is why he broke from the medieval tradition wherein this eclogue, through Servius' interpretation of it, became the prediction of the birth of Christ (and which made Virgil almost a Christian). Does this, then, represent a sort of blasphemy, or lack of *buen gusto*? The Christian interpretation was accepted by some in the eighteenth century, and most probably, at least in some places, still endures today. The answer to this question is, I believe, that Encina did not "break" with "medieval" tradition: that had been done by the humanists before him, and by Nebrija. The philological studies of the classic (and sacred) texts brought a new light, and a feeling of modernity, to the interpretations of the text. Encina also provides an explanation of sorts when he says that Virgil predicted this birth, and avoids the blasphemous comparison by emphasizing the fulfillment of the prediction through the greatness and goodness of the times in *Spain* (which word later he will use to translate "mundum") since the birth of Prince John. One may still ask how Queen Isabella felt about this. Perhaps she, like Nebrija, or because of him, was "modern" in these matters of classical literature. [9]

---

[9] Erasmus, in an epistle to Henry Bullock, mocked the critics of his version—*corrected*—of the New Testament. The question of blasphemy and parody at this time has been discussed by María Rosa Lida de Malkiel, "La hipérbole sagrada en la poesía castellana del siglo XV," *Revista de Filología Hispánica*, VIII (1946), 122, cited in Gillet, IV. 341; Joseph E. Gillet, in his ed. of Torres Naharro, Vol. IV (Philadelphia, 1961), "Torres Naharro and the Drama of the Renaissance," especially the subsection "The Deification of Women"; and Otis H. Green, *Spain and the Western Tradition*, IV (Madison, 1968), especially Ch. 7, "Truancy and Recantation," among others. Well-known is the poem of Montoro dedicated to Queen Isabella:

> Si no pariera Sanctana
> hasta ser nacida vos,
> de vos el hijo de Dios
> rescibiera carne humana.

Encina's translation may be judged as approaching this hyperbole to some extent. Montoro's poem did, in fact, provoke the condemnation of some other poets of the time. Mrs. Malkiel sees the phenomenon of blasphemy (in a much broader perspective than indicated here) as a reflection of a deep-rooted fissure, related to the problem of the *conversos*, who contributed to "el desorden íntimo y...la confusión de jerarquías espirituales, de suyo existente en toda la sociedad de la tardía Edad Media." Such a

As far as the Christian element of this eclogue goes, however, we must note one difference between this and the previous eclogues (but not all the subsequent ones): where Virgil utilizes pagan, or classical, mythology, Encina either converts this into Christian mythology and terminology (mostly the latter) or simply ignores it. He does not do so here. For one thing, we may state that when Encina used the *verso de arte mayor*, classical mythology was a substance built into it. The Muses of Sicily, moreover, can, I think, be easily associated with the Cumaean Sibyll of line four of Virgil—and this is definitely a "Christian" element in Virgil's poem which Encina could not have missed. In the first *Cancionero* poem "La natividad de nuestro salvador" we read, along with many Biblical references, a series of Sibylline predictions, including the following:

> Dixo Sibila Cumana
> gran orden comiença ya,
> que de la Virgen verná
> la prosapia soberana: (fo. [10]ᵛ)

On the same folio we read the prophecy of "Sibila Pérsica" that through the Virgin will become "el invisible apalpado," which is confusing in this connection since he states in the eclogue "Ni a todos tampoco [agradan] las cosas palpables." The confusion is Encina's, and I will suggest that it comes from his using *arte mayor*. [10] Note the words "gran orden comiença" also in his translation of Virgil.

---

conclusion does not apply here, certainly, although Encina's translation of the fourth eclogue deserves consideration in this respect; neither would I apply Mrs. Malkiel's conclusion to a blasphemous poem of Encina's, "A una señora que le dio un regoxo de pan" (fo. 83), where the love offering of a piece of bread is compared metaphorically to the Eucharist, e.g., "pan de passión," "en pan os mostrastes."

[10] In the *Cancionero* of 1496 there are, in addition to the fourth Virgilian eclogue, three other pieces in *arte mayor*: "Triunfo de fama" (written upon the completion of his translations of Virgil), and two dedications, one to the Duke and Duchess of Alba after he entered their service, and one to D. Gutierre de Toledo (who was responsable for Encina's appointment). In a word, they are poor examples of his art. In particular, attention should be paid to his "Tragedia..." (probably 1497; included in the facs. ed.) and his last-known work, "Trivagia" (1519). The "Tragedia" was written on the death of Prince John—to whom he had

The tradition of Servius, then, is not only known by Encina, but, in a manner of speaking, utilized by him in the long religious poem on the birth of Christ. (The Sybilline Oracles, of course, had long been a part of the Christian tradition.) Encina departs from this tradition in the fourth eclogue, and (if this sort of thing really can be determined in poetry) does so without embarrassment. Virgil, the great poet of antiquity, no longer is associated with Christian interpretations. Perhaps Encina was taught, perhaps by Nebrija, that the Christian interpretation was a pious one, but untenable by *modern* standards of philology and criticism (and theology?). The matter of correcting long-standing errors in texts and the interpretations of them had been going on for quite some time, and extended as well to sacred texts. (Nebrija, as an outstanding philologist, a few years later was to work on the polyglot Bible.)

What we will notice here is a "higher style," which Encina promised at the beginning (Cantemos estilo notable a notables)— Virgil intended merely to write of higher things (actually, *slightly* higher: *paulo* maiora). We will find in this fourth eclogue of Encina's, then, a great deal of Juan de Mena and a great deal of fifteenth-century terminology, such as *grandes primores*, where Virgil speaks merely of hedgerow and tamarisk; or "cosas palpables," of which Virgil does not speak.

We see one excellent example of how Encina incorporates both classical and Christian motives in his translation of "Virgo."

---

dedicated the *Arte de poesía* as well as his translations of Virgil; there is no reason to doubt the sincerity of his anguish, but its expression in this poem is not successful. His "Trivagia" describes his voyage to Jerusalem, where he celebrated his first mass. He barely observes the fact (one line), but devotes an excessive amount of space to meals he and his travelling companions enjoyed. A typical example from it [*Viage y Peregrinación que hizo y escribió...J. de la E....de Jerusalém* (Madrid, 1786), p. 42]:

> Comimos, bebimos, como hombres golosos:
> Después que de vino ración nos fue dada,
> Dormida la siesta, caída y pasada,
> Que de lo pasado muy bien reposamos,
> Los unos, los otros nos aparejamos,
> Al Santo Sepulcro hacer nuestra entrada.

I do not wish to denigrate Encina here, but rather to combine objectivity with admiration for the felicities that do occur in this fourth eclogue.

He transposes, first of all, the references to Virgo and Saturnia, so that Virgo can be incorporated in the same strophe with its classical meaning, "justicia," as well as its obvious Christian one, "Virgen María."

There are some interesting grammatical and structural changes in the above strophes. Virgil's lines are not particularly balanced in a rhetorical way (the matter of his form aside, of course). There is a parallelism of sorts in "si canimus silvas, silvae sunt consule dignae," in "iam redit et Virgo, redeunt Saturnia regna," and, less so, in the repetitive and emphatic "iam" (which will be continued by Virgil throughout the poem). Encina has many examples of parallelisms, or formal balance, including contrasts. In his first line "musas" and "pastores"; in lines three and four a contrast between "razón" and "misterios"; in the following two lines both a rhetorical parallelism and a formal contrast, as well as in the last two lines, each of which begins with an imperative, "cantemos" and "y suene." This may be seen, to a somewhat lesser extent, in the following two strophes as well ("Los bienes comiençan, los males fenecen," etc.)

Changes are seen in the previously mentioned inversion of "Virgo" and "Saturnia," and in particular in Encina's changing the tone and intent of several of Virgil's lines. "Cumaei" gives way to the more general "Sibila"; Virgil's somewhat ambiguous statement "Ultima Cumaei...etc." becomes the definite "*Según*... etc.," and amidst the many imperative forms that Encina uses we find the indicative "merecen," which does not correspond to Virgil's "*sint*...*dignae*."

Unlike Virgil, Encina shows no trace of "rustic" terms: Virgil mentions both "arbusta" and "myricae," but Encina uses only the word, a Latinate one, "silvas," and depends otherwise on abstract terms—"primores," "menores."

tu modo nascenti puero, quo ferrea primum
desinet ac toto surget gens aurea mundo,
casta fave Lucina: tuus iam regnat Apollo.
teque adeo decus hoc aevi, te consule, inibit,
Pollio, et incipient magni procedere menses;
te duce, si qua manent sceleris vestigia nostri,
inrita perpetua solvent formidine terras.
ille deum vitam accipiet divisque videbit

permixtos heroas et ipse videbitur illis,
pacatumque reget patriis virtutibus orbem.

Al rey y reyna

O rey Don Hernando y Doña Ysabel,
en vos començaron los siglos dorados;
serán todo tiempo los tiempos nombrados
que fueren regidos por vuestro nivel:
tenéys él y vos y assí vos como él
con Dios tanta fe, que sus deservicios
avéys destruydo y todos los vicios
y alguno si queda daréys cabo dél.

Biváys muchos años acá en este suelo
reynando y saliendo con quanto quisierdes,
mas ya Dios queriendo después que partierdes
coronas de reyes avréys en el cielo:
avréys con los santos su mesmo consuelo
gozando en presencia la vista de Dios,
y el príncipe acá después ya de vos
los reynos seguros terná sin recelo.

The comparison of a translation with its original, even when the former is meant to be as accurate and literal as possible, is a difficult thing; in Encina, where the process is entirely different, the problems are also different. In reading these ten lines of Virgil alongside the two strophes of Encina, one perceives the gist of the matter that runs through the two poems, but it does not seem much more than that. Immediately it is apparent that Encina has transmuted the whole context while maintaining only certain semantic elements (not paraphrastic). "Començaron los siglos dorados" certainly corresponds to "toto surget gens aurea mundo." But there is a change: "En vos" refers to the parents of the child, not the child himself. Virgil tells Pollio that he will have glory because of this child; Encina speaks of the glory that is already the Catholic monarchs'. Of Virgil Encina has dropped totally "tu modo [nascenti puero]...casta fave Lucina: tuus iam regnat Apollo," and the concept "et incipient magni procedere menses." In Encina we find almost four lines which, while in the spirit of

Virgil, do not correspond semantically (i.e., literally): "Tenéys él y vos y assí vos como él / con Dios tanta fe," and "Biváys muchos años acá en este suelo / reynando y saliendo con quanto quisierdes."

Menéndez y Pelayo calls this a parody (at times), and Mayáns is condemning. (Menéndez y Pelayo does not condemn; for Mayáns see Andrews, p. 34 f.) Encina directs himself to the Catholic monarchs, praises them less obliquely than Virgil does Pollio; yet every concept of Virgil, except that mentioned above, finds its way, usually semantically, into Encina's translation. What Encina adds—that is not quite the word—in no way differs from Virgil's intent.

Encina is less polished. Don Quixote, using a proverb as was his wont from time to time (as it was Virgil's) asked Sancho where he had been taught to speak of the rope in the house of the man who had been hanged. In the "Consolación" that Encina wrote on the death of a friend's mother he stated he was certain she was forgiven her sins, having confessed them on her death bed; he—Encina—was certain in his *Tragedia* that Prince John went to heaven ("que yo cierto creo," he said). And here, too, in spite of the Christian contemplation of death so common in the fifteenth century, Encina might have tempered this section a bit by dwelling less on the certainty of the death of the King and Queen. Virgil does not do that; Virgil is too polished. He says that the unborn child—Encina's Don Juan—will receive the life of the gods, etc., and he will rule the earth. Compare Virgil's last three lines and Encina's last strophe. But Encina can be most "polished," particularly in these translations. Again we do have the *arte mayor* at hand to offer as an explanation for some apparent lapses.

At tibi prima, puer, nullo munuscula cultu
errantes hederas passim cum baccare tellus
mixtaque ridenti colocasia fundet acantho.
ipsae lacte domum referent distenta capellae
ubera, nec magnos metuent armenta leones;
ipsa tibi blandos fundent cunabula flores.

Al príncipe

A vos, principado, por daros holgança
en vuestra niñez la tierra os dará
yedras y nardos y más mezclará
acanto y más plantas sin darle labrança:
las cabras darán muy gran abundança,
las tetas tendidas con leche a montones;
no temerá nadie los grandes leones,
avrá muchas flores en vuestra criança.

occidet et serpens, et fallax herba veneni
occidet; Assyrium volgo nascetur amomum.
At simul heroum laudes et facta parentis
iam legere et quae sit poteris cognoscere virtus,
molli paulatim flavescet campus arista,
incultisque rubens pendebit sentibus uva
et durae quercus sudabunt roscida mella.

Ninguna ponçoña podrá ponçoñar,
ninguna serpiente avrá ponçoñosa,
será destruyda la yerva engañosa,
podremos do quiera de amomo gozar:
después que mayor sabréys ya mirar
los hechos antiguos y de vuestro padre,
la gran ecelencia de vuestra gran madre;
veréys las virtudes, sabréys las obrar.

Yréys poco a poco creciendo y mostrando
cordura, saber, virtud y bondad;
los campos darán de su voluntad
nacidos los panes creciendo y tostando:
las çarças y espinas, las uvas colgando
de grandes razimos muy mucho cargadas,
maduras y dulces, no siendo labradas,
los robles muy duros, las mieles sudando.

Encina's three strophes follow Virgil directly, concept for concept
(semantically and literally), with the exception of Virgil's "colo-
casia" and "baccare." Where Virgil offers "*assyrium* amomum"
Encina provides "amomo" simply. Perhaps these are flowers

unknown to Encina. This "flower strophe" offers some insights to
Encina's aesthetics. Virgil says the earth will offer you ivy;
Encina says the earth will give you ivy "por daros holgança."
(My eighteenth-century Virgil explains this in a note: "He
promises him Ivy as a future Poet..." p. 19.) Encina says the
earth will offer "yedras y nardos, y más mezclará / acanto y más
plantas..." unlike Virgil but very much like Juan de Mena. This
vague redundancy is, I feel, less a poetic device, as Mrs. Malkiel
has implied in her study of Juan de Mena, than a poetic fallacy,
which I have also called a poetic-linguistic complacency.

There are two examples here of Encina's prolixity, which is
frequently distasteful in him. They are each very different types.
"Occidet et serpens" becomes very extended: "Ninguna ponço-
ñosa podrá ponçoñar, / ninguna serpiente avrá ponçoñosa." If these
lines are not pleasing—indeed, if they are not what we now call
"good"—one recognizes immediately Encina's intent. "Incultique
rubens pendebit sentibus uva" offers even to the most incipient
reader of Virgil an exquisite sensuality of sound that seduces one
to appreciate the *sense* of plump, bold grapes hanging in weighted
clusters. Encina has too many words and no impact: "Las uvas
colgando / de grandes razimos muy mucho cargadas, / maduras y
dulces, no siendo labradas." (But see two strophes above: las tetas
tendidas con leche a montones.")

Encina in his second strophe is much more positive than Virgil:
"Después que mayor sabréys...[y] *veréys* las virtudes;" "At
simul...*quae sit poteris cognoscere virtus.*" (Note subjunctive *sit*
compared to Encina's future indicative. I believe Encina changed
Virgil's tenses and moods quite consciously. See the preceding
segment where he does follow Virgil, using "serán" corresponding
to "inibit.")

Encina, I have suggested, wrote (or "translated") these eclogues
with three purposes: 1) to present Virgil to those who did not
know him (or could not read him); 2) to offer for public reading
a series of ten well-wrought poems praising the Catholic Kings;
3) to please especially those few whose knowledge of Virgil was
intimate and whose love of Spanish poetry was great. There have
been many examples of this, some of which have been touched
on. But in the first strophe above we have a superlative example
of this. Compare: "At tibi *prima*, puer,..." and "A vos, *princi-*

pado." Encina was "irreverent" (to use Menéndez y Pelayo's term) only in the sense that he did not think Virgil was divine. For him, Virgil (along with Juan de Mena) was the greatest poet of the past. (Also Dante and Petrarch, he might have added out of politeness: but these were not the dominating figures in *lyric* poetry that they would soon come to be in Spain.) Surely the Queen would have enjoyed these lines; but it is very unlikely she would have had that special thrill that Antonio de Nebrija must have felt when he read "principado" and admired the stunning "trope." [11] It is very possible that Nebrija admired intensely his pupil's *verso de arte mayor*. Times change as quickly as decades; today there are few who enjoy the poetry of Juan de Mena. And yet, it must be said: Encina's translation of Virgil's fourth eclogue is not very good poetry. But in spots it is good, and the present "spot" offers several fine examples. Virgil's "ipsae lacte domum referent distenta capellae / ubera" provides a splendid metaphor for Encina (after a nondescript start): "Las cabras darán muy gran abundança, / las tetas tendidas con leche a montones." Having recognized Encina's careful and sensitive understanding of Virgil, it is impossible to suspect him of a misreading; nonetheless he far exceeds Virgil's intention in one hyperbole of his here. Virgil's "et durae quercus sudabunt roscida mella" is, I am sure, an example of how Virgil never—or rarely—says *more* than the image requires: he means an oak tree in which the bees have harvested their honey. Encina translates exactly: "Los robles muy duros, las mieles sudando." It is true to Virgil, but in Encina it is also very fanciful because he has very definitely entered the field of fantasy four lines earlier: "Nacidos los panes creciendo y tostando," the key words being "panes" and "tostando." Virgil says realistically that the corn in the fields will turn yellow.

Pauca tamen suberunt prisca vestigia fraudis,
quae temptare Thetim ratibus, quae cingere muris
oppida, quae iubeant telluri infindere sulcos.
alter erit tum Tiphys, et altera quae vehat Argo
delectos heroas; erunt etiam altera bella
atque iterum ad Troiam magnus mittetur Achilles.

---

[11] See my discussion above (Virgil, II, l. 45 ff. ["Huc ades, o formose puer"].

Algunas pisadas del mal ya passado
podrá ser que queden de aquel siglo duro,
que manden lugares cercarse de muro
y pongan las naves por mar en cuydado:
y hagan hazer con reja y arado
los surcos hendidos por baxo de tierra;
otro Tyfis y Argo será, y otra guerra,
y otro gran Achiles a Troya embiado.

Hinc ubi iam firmata virum te fecerit aetas,
cedet et ipse mari vector, nec nautica pinus
mutabit merces; omnis feret omnia tellus.
non rastros patietur humus, non vinea falcem;

Después que la edad más hombre os hiziere,
ni avrá marinero ni nave ninguna;
terná cada tierra tan buena fortuna,
que tenga abundança de quanto quisiere:
entonces la tierra, qualquiera que fuere,
no avrá menester de ser ya labrada,
ni viña ninguna de ser ya podada;
darán tan buen fruto qual hombre pidiere.

robustus quoque iam tauris iuga solvet arator;
nec varios discet mentiri lana colores,
ipse sed in pratis aries iam suave rubenti
murice, iam croceo mutabit vellera luto;
sponte sua sandyx pascentes vestiet agnos.
'Talia saecla' suis dixerunt 'currite' fusis
concordes stabili fatorum numine Parcae.

Y entonces tan bien qualquier labrador
soltará sus bueyes sin darles más pena;
no avrá menester el yugo y melena,
dexarlos ha libres de toda lavor:
no avrá ya tintura de ningún color,
no avrá menester teñirse la lana,
el mesmo carnero de púrpura y grana
terná vellocino teñido y con flor.

Tan bien los corderos serán revestidos
de aquella color qual yerva pacieren,

> color sandicino si sandís comieren,
> de su natural sin tinta teñidos:
> con firme concierto, los hados movidos,
> dixeron conformes las Parcas fatales,
> "hilemos los siglos agora ya tales
> que buelvan de nuevo dorados polidos."

Encina is working in a double and particularly difficult "artistic restraint" here. One part is that of the *arte mayor* (always "difficult" for him—and in the *Trivagia* his preoccupation with the form seems to have left unbridled his inhibitions insofar as confession of his previous faults is concerned, and insofar as his real, exceedingly human and not very religious nature is concerned. It may be remembered that our poet spent more time "talking" —the *Trivagia* is a very prosaic piece—about lunch and dinner than the celebration of his first mass or his entrance into the temple built on the site of Christ's crucifixion.) The other part of this restraint is his working in a translation. Whether this is the explanation or not of his mode of expression in the first strophe, nonetheless the strophe offers the possibility of a psychological interpretation.

In Encina's first line there is a double vagueness: "tan bien" [también] and "qualquier." "También" is a translation of "quoque"; "qualquier" is his own substitute for Virgil's "robustus," a term that I am certain he could have worked into his translation without difficulty. It may be merely that he considers "robustus" too "rustic," but he does use "labrador." We see in the first strophe above a parallelism, "no avrá menester," "no avrá ya tintura," "no avrá menester," which, in this method I am following for the moment, reveals another formalistic pattern, perhaps taken from Virgil's triple "iam" here. Encina follows Virgil's "tauris iuga solvet arator," but he adds "sin darles más *pena*"; and for emphasis perhaps, "no avrá menester el yugo y melena." Following this is the line "Dexarlos ha libres de toda lavor." None of this is found in Virgil literally. Encina is speaking of the "Golden Age," which he belonged to—or which he desired to belong to. Then comes the following line of Encina, which is not found in Virgil either: "No avrá tintura de ningún color." An interpretation of this in regard to Encina is very easy; the idea has been touched on before in connection with his use of social metaphors.

In the line "No avrá menester teñirse la lana," the repeated "no avrá menester" in this case is supposed to correspond to Virgil's frank "mentire." Sometimes harsh (when speaking about his "detratores," or to Bárbola), usually Encina is very mild in his lyric aspect, and this does not permit "mentire" where "no avrá *menester*" will do.

One will notice in others of Encina's works (the "Disparates" notably) a high level of fantastic writing—this is a contrast to his more usual, controlled writing. Here I believe, we may observe a curious combination of the fantastic and the literal in him. Virgil's "sponte sua sandyx *pascentes* vestiet agnos" may suggest, but does not say so literally, Encina's "serán revestidos / de aquella color qual yerva pacieren." He builds on this: "color sandicino si sandís comieren," which is a very *literal* explanation of his fantasy. Then—worthy of Jules Verne!—he adds that "el mesmo carnero de púrpura y grana / terná vellocino teñido *y con flor.*" This is not a misinterpretation of "croceo." This is similar to his fantastic elaboration in the last segment discussed above.

Adgredere o magnos (aderit iam tempus) honores
cara deum suboles, magnum Iovis incrementum!
aspice convexo nutantem pondere mundum
terrasque tractusque maris caelumque profundum;
aspice venturo laetantur ut omnia saeclo!

> O claro linage, vitoria escogida,
> los grandes triunfos y mucha alabança
> a vos que se deve se dé sin dudança,
> ya vienen los tiempos de gloria crecida:
> mirad toda España que estava perdida,
> las tierras y el mar, la fe no constante,
> alégrense todos por lo de adelante,
> que el bien se nos viene con vuestra venida.

In practical terms the above lines of both poets correspond closely. A nice touch is Encina's avoiding the too-pagan "magnum Iovis incrementum" and also "deum suboles" in his "vitoria escogida." Encina's last line is in excess of the original, but easily accomoda-

ted; Virgil's "aspice...*mundum*" becomes "mirad toda *España*."
Virgil's statement "aspice...(ut) *laetantur*" becomes "Alégrense"—
with reference in Encina to the "tierras" and "mar," but which
in Virgil is also "caelum." It is curious that Encina should break
this parallel construction, for we could well imagine land, sea and
sky (or even more likely, heaven) rejoicing. Encina here provides
a contrast, lacking in Virgil, with the past, and adds the element
"la fe no constante," bothersome here, because when he returns
to the "present" in "alégrense todos" "fe no constante" is perforce
included with "tierras" and "mar."

o mihi tum longae maneat pars ultima vitae,
spiritus et, quantum sat erit tua dicere facta:
non me carminibus vincat nec Thracius Orpheus,
nec Linus, huic mater quamvis atque huic pater adsit,
Orphei Calliopea, Lino formosus Apollo.

> O Dios, quién pudiesse bivir tantos días
> que bien vuestros hechos pudiesse contar;
> ni Orfeo ni Lino podría ygualar
> comigo tan dulces cantando armonías:
> aunque sabemos de sus melodías,
> y Orfeo ser hijo de Caliopea,
> y a Lino su padre Apolo le sea,
> en esto les puedo llevar mejorías.

Encina enters the spirit of this very well, and strives to equal
Virgil as well as Orpheus and Linos in melodic lines. The sonic
contrast in the two hemistiches "Y Orfeo *ser* hijo" and "Y a Lino
su padre" is superb, and the unusually extreme hyperbaton in
"comigo tan dulces cantando armonías" is equally so.

Pan etiam, Arcadia mecum si iudice certet,
Pan etiam Arcadia dicat se iudice victum.
incipe, parve puer, risu cognoscere matrem:
matri longa decem tulerunt fastidia menses.
incipe, parve puer: cui non risere parenti,
nec deus hunc mensa, dea nec dignata cubili est.

> Y aquel Pan Cilenio si quiere su vez [sic]
> comigo apostar yo tengo creydo
> que él mesmo a sí mesmo se dé por vencido

y aun siendo entre nos Arcadia juez:
o niño gracioso, en vuestra niñez
riendo mostrad plazer desde agora;
quitad los fastidios de vuestra señora,
pagadle el trabajo del parto y preñez.

Fin

Mostradle comienço de bienes estraños,
pues deven los hijos gran deuda a las madres;
que a los que no toman plazer con sus padres,
aquellos da Dios trabajos y daños;
comiencen verdades, feneçan engaños,
feneçan pesares, comiencen plazeres;
o reyna tan santa, primor de mugeres,
o rey ecelente, biváys dos mil años.

One wishes Encina had sustained himself. His first four lines here
are pale in comparison with the daring ones before them. He ends
on his own note, repeating in a way his earlier "los bienes
comiençan, los males fenecen" from the second strophe. (It might
prove interesting to observe more carefully the many discrepancies
in mood between Encina and Virgil in this eclogue, i.e., between
imperative and indicative, and sometimes subjunctive.) The last
line, hearty as it is, is both familiar (the fifth strophe of this poem,
for one example) and more than a little pedestrian.

    This is Encina's "estilo notable." It is not quite satisfying—and
yet it is often clever; on a certain level it is sometimes excellent
(for those whose knowledge of Virgil is intimate); and on its own
merits it occasionally offers a line or two that is brilliant. And,
most certainly, we must not forget that one of our poets is Juan
del Encina and the other—the other is Virgil. *Non me carminibus
vincat.*

APPENDIX

A los muy esclarecidos y siempre vitoriosos príncipes, Don Hernando y Doña Ysabel. Comiença el prólogo en la translación de las Bucólicas de Virgilio por Juan del Enzina. [12]

La grandeza de vuestras hazañas, dinas de imortalidad, muy altos y muy poderosos reyes, despierta las lenguas de los dormidos coraçones y no dexa tener sufrimiento para que puedan callar avn los que hablar no saben. Mas, ¿quién será tan dino, por mucho

---

[12] a) My purpose in reprinting the Dedications is partly to present Encina's comments on pastoral poetry but mostly to show Encina's consideration of himself. He may be a humble subject of the Catholic Monarch, but he associates himself with the very best: Virgil, Homer, St. Jerome, Moses, God, etc. This will support my observations (following Andrews, see Note 4 above) in the analysis of his translations of how he weaves himself into the *Eclogues* as a major character.

b) This is not the place for any but the briefest observation of Encina's prose. The Dedications were reprinted by Menéndez y Pelayo (*Antología de poetas líricos castellanos*) but not from the first ed. Substantially, the present text is the same as Menéndez y Pelayo's; I have preserved the orthography, but have resolved abbreviations, supplied accents and revised the punctuation of the 1496 ed. Encima's comments on poetic form in his "Arte de poesía" and elsewhere draw our attention to the comparative stiffness of his prose. Although not incapable of graceful periods and rhetorical felicities, Encina does not write sustained passages of good prose. I observe the intriguing question of punctuation in texts printed in gothic type, which causes some difficulties in reading Encina's poetry, and which I touch upon in the present study. Encina employs a period [.] and a colon [:], but I do not perceive any consistent difference between them. (I have used periods, commas and semi-colons, following Encina's leads but making no attempt to be consistent or faithful.) We observe the excessive conjunctions (y; mas), which seem to be Encina's major device for making transitions in prose, not unlike the style of the times, but not the style of a master; in his poetry he did not encounter this difficulty,

saber que alcance, que deva tener confiança en su ingenio para dinamente llegar a contar el menor quilate de las ecelencias de vuestra real magestad, cuanto más yo, que aún agora soy nuevo en las armas y muy flaco para navegar por el gran mar de vuestras alabanças. O invitíssimos príncipes, ¡quién supiesse recontar las vitorias y trivnfos que en los reynos por vuestra mano conquistados avéys recebido! Que no solamente el reyno de Granada, mas avn el vuestro de Castilla, casi todo ganastes con fuerça de armas, queriendo Dios ayudaros. Y avnque aquesto agora nos parece mucho, es cierto después nos parecerá casi nada en comparación de las vitorias que os están guardadas. Pues, ¿qué diré de vuestra poderosa justicia y con cuánta paz y sossiego vuestros reynos son regidos, hallando como los hallastes tan estragados que según el gran daño que en ellos estava no se esperava remedio? Y sobre todo nuestra fe, que ya estava puesta en despeñadero donde muchos deslizavan, vosotros, christianíssimos reyes, la restaurastes y esclarecistes, que quiso Dios escogeros para remedio de tantos males. Vosotros soys la cumbre de todos los príncipes y reyes, adonde la fe y la justicia se conoce bien quien son; adonde la manificencia tiene sus fuerças enteras, soys la mesma liberalidad en las cosas que lícitamente podéys usar della. No sé para qué me pongo en alabaros, pues entrar por este camino es querer agotar el mar, ni mi saber me da lugar para ello.

---

owing, I believe, to the structure of the genre as well as his accomplishments as a musician. I have supplied some capitalization for titles (e.g., De rebus rusticis) but have followed Encina's own usage elsewhere (e.g., biblia, sagrada escritura, Dios, Oracio, Insula cóo, etc.). Paragraphing is mine.

c) This is not a philological study of the Dedications, but I draw attantion to some words, especially when these differ from Menéndez y Pelayo's readings. I indicate them "[sic]," without comment. One item may merit attention: In the Dedication to the Monarchs I note, following Menéndez y Pelayo, the declaration "avémosla de tomar como razones pastoriles así simplemente dichas." The text splits a / si by a line runover. Normally, Encina uses assi; a reading "razones pastoriles a sí simplemente [i.e., basically, innocently, with no intent to offend] dichas" may be valid and is the one I offer; it seems to me a more decisive statement about his use of the content and motifs of Virgil's poetry (see the Second Eclogue in particular) than Menéndez y Pelayo's reading. However, it must be noted that when a line runover splits ss, one s is consistently dropped; it is, therefore, a question again of punctuation rather than of the transcription of the text.

Mas como el desseo de servir a vuestra alteza sea mayor que el temor de descubrir mis defetos, aunque grandes, no quiero escusarme de salir a barrera y ensayarme primero en algún baxo estilo y más convenible a mi ingenio, para después escrivir algo de vuestras istorias en otro estilo más alto, si en ello mostráys serviros. Y por que mi desseo consiga efeto más concertado, acordé dedicaros las Bucólicas de Virgilio, que es la primera de sus obras, adonde habla de pastores, siguiendo como dize el Donato la orden de los mortales, cuyo exercicio primeramente fue guardar ganados manteniéndose de frutas silvestres, y después siguióse la agricultura, y andando más el tiempo nacieron batallas. Y en esta manera el estilo del gran Homero mantuano en sus tres obras principales procedió, de las cuales por agora para entrada y preludio de mi propósito, estas Bucólicas quise trasladar, trobadas en estilo pastoril, aplicándolas a los muy loables hechos de vuestro reynar según parece en el argumento de cada vna.

Y dexadas otras muchas razones que a ello me movieron, parecióme ser deuda muy conocida a tales príncipes y reyes que tan gran primado y ecelencia tienen sobre todos los otros, se huviesse de consagrar y dirigir obra de tan gran poeta, a quien el nuestro Quintiliano da la palma entre los latinos y esso mesmo Macobrio y Servio y todos los que se pusieron a cotejar los estilos poéticos. Y assí como haziendo mención de poeta sin añedir otro nombre entendemos de Virgilio por ecelencia, assí es mucha razón que haziendo mención de reyes por ecelencia entendamos de vuestra real corona. ¿Quién uvo que tan gran magestad de palabras alcançase como Virgilio? ¿Qué sentencia o qué seta de filósofos uvo que él no comprehendiesse? No sin mérito dizen Cicerón averle llamado segunda esperança de Roma cuando en su mocedad pronunciaua ciertos versos en el teatro romano.

No tengáys por mal, manánimos príncipes, en dedicaros obra de pastores, pues que no ay nombre más convenible al estado real; del qual nuestro redentor que es el verdadero rey de los reyes se precia mucho según parece en muchos lugares de la sagrada escritura. Y las alabanças de la vida pastoril, no sólo Virgilio y otros poetas, más aún Plinio, gravíssimo autor, las pone en el décimo otauo libro de la natural estoria hablando muy largamente de la vida rústica y no menos de agricultura; y testigo es Catón el mayor en el libro De rebus rusticis adonde dize que cuando antiguamente alabauan algún hombre, llamávanle buen labrador. Y aún los poetas y hombres dotos desseavan lugares apartados assí como bosques y montes y otras silvas y arboledas, y con este desseo dezía Virgilio: O qui me sistat in uallibus hemi.

Mas tornando agora en mí, quiero saber quién me traxo en tan gran cuydado que a reyes tan ecelentes mi pluma osasse llevar nuevas de mi desseo; que no soy dino para ponerme en aplicar esta obra a vuestros tan altos primores. ¡O quántas vezes me paro a pensar desconfiando de mi ingenio, quién me puso en este trabajo aviendo otros muchos que muy mejor que yo lo pudieran tomar! Mas consuélome con aquello que dize Tulio en el libro De perfeto oratore a Marco bruto, diziendo que ninguno deve desespar [sic] de trabajar en las letras, y si no pudiere llegar al más alto escalón, llegará al segundo o tercero o quarto, que en tiempo de Homero fueron otros aunque no tan notables. Y esso mesmo quando Archiloco y Sófocles y Píndaro florecieron, no faltaron otros que escriviessen aunque no pudieron bolar tan alto; que ni el gran estilo de Platón espantó a Aristóteles; ni el mesmo Aristóteles a otros muchos sin cuento; ni Demóstenes que fue el más ecelente orador de Grecia espantó a otros algunos de su tiempo. Y no solamente fue esto en las artes ecelentes, mas aún entre los maestros de otras obras, según parece en los pintores que aunque no pudieron imitar la hermosura de una ymagen que estava en Rodas ni la de Venus que estava en la Insula có ni la de Júpiter olímpico, no por esso dexaron de pintar. Y assí yo aunque mi obra no mereça ser muy alabada en perfeción, a lo menos no dexaré de tentar vados para ver si podré alcançar algún poco de loor con esfuerço de aquellas palabras que Virgilio dize: Tentanda via est qua me quoque possim tollere humo, uictorque uirum volitare per ora.

Y muchas dificultades hallo en la tradución de aquesta obra por el gran defeto de vocablos que ay en la lengua castellana en comparación de la latina, de donde se causa en muchos lugares no poderles dar la propria sinificación; quanto más que por razón del metro y consonantes, será forçado algunas vezes de impropriar las palabras, y acrecentar o menguar según hiziere a mi caso. Y aún muchas razones avrá que no se puedan traer al propósito, mas aquellas tales según dize Servio avémoslas de tomar como razones pastoriles a sí, simplemente dichas; y si fuere necessario, usar de aquello que usan los eclesiásticos diziendo un salmo por vn solo verso que haze al caso de la fiesta. Mas en quanto yo pudiere y mi saber alcançare, siempre procuraré seguir la letra aplicándola a vuestras más que reales personas, y endereçando parte dello al nuestro muy esclarecido príncipe don Juan, vuestro bien aventurado hijo, y atribuyendo cada cosa al que mejor se pudiere atribuyr. Y aunque en los más de los lugares no hable sino del uno, será por más verdaderamente seguir al poeta y por que son vuestras virtudes y ecelencias tan pareadas y puestas en unidad, que no se pueden tocar las del uno sin que suenen las del otro. Y pues el grandíssimo desseo de servir a vuestra alteza me puso en este cuydado, con aquella humildad y acatamiento que devo, suplico a vuestra real magestad quiera recebir este pequeño presente de su siervo con aquellas manos triunfales y vulto sereno con que ilustra toda la monarchía de España y modera y rige la ocidental región y con que combida a su amistad no solamente a los príncipes de la religión cristiana, mas aún a gran parte de la barbárica gente.

Al muy esclarecido y bien aventurado príncipe don Juan. Comiença el prólogo en la translación de las Bucólicas de Virgilio por Juan del Enzina.

Suelen aquellos que dan obra a las letras, príncipe muy ecelente, esperimentar sus ingenios en trasladar libros y autores griegos en lengua latina; y assí mesmo los hombres de nuestra nación procuran tomar esperimento de su estudio bolviendo libros de latín en nuestra lengua castellana. Y no solamente los hombres de mediano saber, mas aún entre otros varones muy dotos, no rehusó aqueste exercicio Tulio, puesto en la cumbre de todos los ingenios, que bolvió a la lengua latina muchas obras griegas ya perdidas por negligencia de nuestros antecessores, principalmente aquellas muy altas oraciones de Esquines y Demóstenes, cuyo argumento parece; las quales nuevamente trasladó Leonardo aretino poco tiempo ha; y la Etica de Aristóteles que agora se lee; y otros libros de Platón. Y aún entre los santos dotores no dio pequeña gloria a san Jerónimo la interpretación y tradución de la biblia. Y en este trabajo se ocuparon Aquila, y Simaco, Teodoción, Orígenes, y Eusebio. Y de los modernos no solamente Leonardo y Filelfo se pusieron a trasladar de una lengua en otra, mas tan bien otros muchos gastaron parte de su tiempo en semejantes exercicios dedicando sus obras a quien su desseo les aconsejava. Y como quiera que yo sea tan desseoso del servicio de vuestra alteza como el que más, con aquella fe que a vuestros claríssimos padres, procurando mostrar algo de mi desseo, en las Bucólicas de Virgilio metí la pluma, temblando con mucha razón, viendo el valer de vuestro gran merecimiento; y amonestado por Oracio en el arte de poesía donde dize los escritores aver de elegir materias yguales a las fuerças de sus ingenios. O bien aventurado príncipe, esperança de las españas, espejo y claridad de tantos reynos, y de muchos más merecedor, ¿quién será tan fuera de sentido que quánto más piense que sabe tanto más no tema escrevir obra de vuestro nombre? No con poco temor mil vezes bolviera las riendas si no me atajara Marcial que en sus epigramas y títulos de baxas obras y entre sus procaces y desvergonçadas palabras entretexía el nombre de Domiciano, el más sobervio y vanaglorioso de los emperadores romanos; el qual pestífero vicio está muy alongado de la real magestad de vuestros padres y vuestra. Assí que con este esfuerço, mi verdadero desseo y vuestras muy claras virtudes me dieron atrevimiento para dirigir y consagrar estas Bucólicas a nuestros muy poderosos reyes, y aplicaros parte dellas, por que creo que en vuestra tierna niñez os avréys exercitado en las obras de aqueste poeta. Y por que favorecéys tanto la ciencia andando acompañado de tan dotíssimos varones, que no menos dexaréys perdurable memoria de aver alargado y estendido los límites y términos de la ciencia que los del imperio.

Mas por no engendrar fastidio a los letores desta mi obra, acordé de la trobar en diversos géneros de metro, y en estilo rústico por consonar con el poeta que introduze personas pastoriles; aunque debaxo de aquella corteza y rústica simplicidad, puso sentencias muy altas y alegóricos sentidos. Y en esta obra se mostró no menos gracioso que doto en la Geórgica, y grave en la Eneyda. Y no en poca estimación era tenida la vida rústica antiguamente, que de allí nacían y se engendravan los varones y capitanes fortíssimos según dize Catón el censorio en su libro de agricultura. Y aquésta fue la que dio nombre a las familias de los Fabios, Pisones, Cicerones, y Léntulos. Y en este exercicio estava ocupado Cincinato quando le denunciaron de parte del senado romano ser criado Ditador, y aún aquesta agricultura sustentava a Marco régulo, cuyo mayordomo muerto, quiso dexar la capitanía y hueste que en Africa governava, por venir a labrar sus tierras; mas el senado y pueblo romano no huvo vergüença de ser su mayordomo y labrarle las tierras. Pues, ¿qué diré de aquel primer justo Abel que guardando estava ganado quando su hermano le mató? Y Noé labrador era; y Abraham, Ysaac, y Jacob con sus doze hijos, pastores fueron; y Moysés en vida pastoril estava metido quando vio aquella visión de la çarça; y David siendo pastor y andando con sus ganados exercitava las fuerças matando ossos y leones y otros fieros animales. Y de allí fue ungido por rey, del qual dixo Dios: Inveni uirum secundum cor meum. Y todos los más de los Patriarcas y Profetas bivieron en semejantes vidas, ni tuvieron por mal muchos grandes filósofos, oradores y poetas rescrevir [sic] de pastores y ornamento del campo. Mas dexados agora todos los otros, assí griegos como latinos que en esta facultad escrivieron libros que a nuestras manos no han venido, yo hallo aquel Marco varrón, a quien santo Agustino en el tercero de la ciudad de dios llama el más enseñado de los romanos, aver escrito de aqueste rústico exercicio siendo de ochenta años assí como él confiessa en el prohemio de una obra que compuso enseñando a su muger cómo labrasse una heredad que avía mercado. Y también Tulio en el De senetute haze mención de las alabanças de la rústica vida; y no menos Paladio ocupó su pluma en semejante estilo. Y assí mesmo Plinio y Columela escrivieron largamente de agricultura, y según ellos dizen, muchos culpan agora a la tierra porque no da tanto fruto como en otro tiempo, y dizen que lo causa estar ya cansada de engendrar; mas estos dos claros varones dañan la tal opinión y afirman ser la causa por que agora las heredades y tierras son labradas por manos de siervos y hombres viles y de baxa suerte, y no dan tanto fruto como quando las labravan aquellas manos que regían las riendas de los carros triunfales; por que entonces con aquel cuydado y diligencia que tratavan las guerras, con aquél labravan el campo. Y de aquí se davan las coronas Cívicas, murales, y obsidionales, gran ornamento de la milicia. Y aquí mandavan las leyes de Ligúrgo [sic] no se criassen los hijos de los Espartanos hasta que fuesen [sic] para tomar armas. Y pues tan ecelentes cosas se siguieron del campo, y tan grandes hombres amaron la agricultura y vida rústica y escrivieron della, no deve ser despreciada mi obra por ser escrita en estilo pastoril.

Y no dudo que mi trabajo sea reprehendido de muchos, por averme puesto a trasladar con mi poco saber obra de tan gran poeta, mayormente atreviéndome a dedicarlo a los más altos príncipes del mundo. Mas los que maliciosos no fueren, no la obra sino la voluntad y desseo deven juzgar; y consuélome con esto, que aún a san Jerónimo en quien ninguna causa de reprehensión avía no faltaron maldizientes y embidiosos que le reprehendiessen, según él se quexa en diversos lugares. Ni menos careció Virgilio de quien le motejase [sic]. Y aún según dize Quintiliano, no se pudo defender Cicerón, en cuyo ingenio las virtudes oratorias y retóricas se encerraron, sin que detratores le tocassen. Mas si vuestra alteza mi baxo servicio manda recebir por suyo, lo qual le suplico con el temor y vergüença que a príncipe tan esclarecido se deve, podrán muy poco dañarme quantos maldizientes biven.